Mission Possible

How God Planted Six Churches In Twelve Months

Mike Napper

Publishing Coordinator – Sharon Kizziah-Holmes
Book Design – Monica Holcomb

INDIE PUB PRESS

Indie Pub Press
Springfield, Missouri

ISBN -13: 978-1-970560-10-7

TABLE OF CONTENTS

Foreword
Preface
Introduction
Chapter 1
   Understanding The Mission Field 1
      1. See What Jesus Sees 2
      2. Know the People, Not Just the Place 3
      3. Walk the Land and Pray 5
      4. Honor the Past, Don't Ignore It 6
      5. Study the Spiritual Climate 6
      6. Clarify Your Calling with Conviction 7
      7. Customize Strategy to the Mission Field 8
      8. Engage and Serve Before You Gather 9
      9. Raise Up Local Leaders Early 10
      10. First 30-Day Field Plan 11
Chapter 2
   Building A Team 14
      1. The Power of Team in the Early Church 15
      2. Who You Build With Matters More Than How Many 16
      3. Pray Your Team Into Place 17
      4. Define Roles Early—Keep Them Flexible 19
      5. Create a Core Team Covenant 21
      6. Prioritize Relationship Over Skill 22
      7. Deal with Conflict Early and Biblically 24
      8. Multiplication Begins with the Core 27
      9. Stories from the Field 28
      10 Questions to Ask as You Build 29
Chapter 3 Securing Resources 31
      1. What Do You Actually Need? 32
      2. Where Does Provision Come From? 35
      3. Fundraising is Discipleship 37
      4. Build a Clear, Credible Budget To Match the Vision .. 39
      5. Set Up Smart Financial Systems 41
      6. Steward What You Have — Then God Sends More 42
      7. Don't Let Finances Dictate Faith 43
      8. Sample Fundraising Script 45

9. Reflection Questions...46

Chapter 4

Spiritual Preparation 47
1. The Spiritual Weight of Church Planting 49
2. Build Yourself Before You Build the Church 50
3. Develop a Personal Prayer Rhythm............................52
4. Invite the Holy Spirit Into Every Step 54
5. Protect Your Soul from Pride and Performance 55
6. Prepare for Spiritual Warfare.....................................56
7. Let God Shape Your Heart for the City......................57
8. Don't Skip the Wilderness..57
9. Key Spiritual Practices 58
10. Ask Others to Cover You 59

Chapter 5

Identifying the Location 61
1. Prayer Must Lead the Process....................................64
2. Start with Mission, Not Map 65
3. Research and Discern 67
5. Consider Strategic Gaps 68
5. Look for People of Peace...69
6. Test It — Don't Just Theorize 69
7. Consider Logistics 71
8. Don't Just Choose a Spot — Claim It Spiritually.........72
9. Be Willing to Pivot..72
10. Plant for the Long Haul 72

Chapter 6

Building Relationships..75
1. Relationships Are the Soil of Discipleship..................76
2. Be Present Before You Promote.................................77
3. Make the First Move...78
4. Start a Culture of Invitation 79
5. Relationships Move at the Speed of Trust...................79
6. Eat Together — Often 80
7. Know Names, Not Just Numbers................................80
8. Lead with Vulnerability..81
9. Create On-Ramps for Community...............................82
10. Build Bridges Before Services..................................83

Chapter 7

    Starting Small 84

        1. Launch with Prayer, Not Pressure 84

        2. Launch at the Right Time 86

        3. Make It a Celebration, Not a Show 88

        4. Promote Relationally, Not Just Digitally....................88

        5. Be Clear on Vision 89

        6. Prepare for Imperfection..89

        7. Prioritize Follow-Up...89

        8. Build for Sustainability, Not Just Launch Day............90

        9. Measure What Matters 91

        10. Celebrate and Evaluate 91

Chapter 8 Making Disciples 93

        1. Build a Disciple-Making Culture, Not Just Programs..94

        2. Start Small to Grow Strong 95

        3. Teach Obedience, Not Just Information 95

        4. Multiply Disciple-Makers 96

        5. Keep It Simple and Reproducible................................96

        6. Center on the Word 98

        7. Make Prayer Central..98

        8. Lead People to Baptism Early 98

        9. Disciple in Real Life..99

        10. Remember: The Spirit is the Discipler 100

Chapter 9

    Developing Leaders..101

        1. Leadership Development Starts with Intentionality ...102

        2. Look for Heart Before Skill.......................................104

        3. Lead by Example 104

        4. Give People Real Responsibility 106

        5. Build Layers of Leadership 107

        6. Create a Simple Leadership Pipeline.........................108

        7. Coach and Develop Continuously 108

        8. Identify and Train Reproducers 109

        9. Be Patient, But Be Persistent.....................................109

        10. Release, Don't Just Retain.......................................110

Chapter 10

    Multiplying Churches...112

        1. Multiplication Starts with Mindset............................113

        2. Build a Sending Culture 116

3. Identify and Equip Planters Early 118
4. Share the Vision Often. 118
5. Develop Reproducible Models 118
6. Partner with Networks and Other Churches 118
7. Send Teams, Not Just Individuals 121
8. Let Go Generously. 122
9. Plan for Sustainability. 123
10. Dream Bigger Than Your Church 123
Chapter 11
Sustaining Momentum. 125
1. Stay Rooted in Prayer 127
2. Keep the Mission Front and Center 128
3. Regularly Reevaluate Systems 129
4. Care for the Core 130
5. Celebrate Small Wins 131
6. Keep Reaching Out. 131
7. Guard Against Mission Drift 132
8. Invest in Next-Level Leaders. 132
9. Renew Vision for Generosity 133
10. Rest Without Losing Momentum 134
Chapter 12
Finishing Well 136
1. Keep Your Eyes on Jesus 137
2. Build What Outlasts You. 138
3. Prepare to Hand It Off 140
4. Stay Faithful Through the Valleys. 141
5. Guard Your Soul. 142
6. Celebrate the Journey 142
7. Leave a Legacy of Sending. 143
8. Let God Define Success. 145
Chapter 13
Overcoming Challenges. 146
1. Spiritual Warfare 147
2. Leadership Fatigue. 148
3. Team Conflict or Disunity 149
4. Financial Shortfalls 150
5. Volunteer Fatigue 150
6. Slow Growth. 150
7. Loss of Key People 151

8. Discouragement and Doubt 152
9. Vision Drift 152
10. Comparison 152

Chapter 14
Establishing a Legacy 155
1. Lead with the End in Mind 156
2. Multiply Disciples, Not Just Churches 156
3. Identify and Train Successors 158
4. Document the Vision 159
5. Develop a Leadership Culture 160
6. Empower Others to Dream 160
7. Build Beyond Your Name 161
8. Think in Generations 161
9. Stay Rooted in the Gospel 161
10. Finish Well 162

Chapter 15
Maintaining Unity Across Churches 163
1. Prioritize Relationships Over Structure 165
2. Repeat Vision and Values Often 167
3. Empower Local Expression 168
4. Stay Theologically Aligned 168
5. Create Rhythms of Connection 168
6. Handle Conflict Biblically 168
7. Share Resources Generously 169
8. Tell the Story Again and Again 170
9. Define What Holds You Together 172
10. Keep the Gospel at the Center 172

Conclusion:
The Call to Multiply 175
This Is a Kingdom Movement 176
You Were Made for This 176
Keep Going 177
Final Prayer 177
Endnotes
Acknowledgments

FOREWORD

Great churches do the basic better than anyone else. They love people and accept them where they and they let God lead them to where they need to be. Great churches develop their people to know Christ and to make Christ known. Great churches pray for each other, encourage each other and sacrifice their resources for the kingdom of God. And great churches worship our great God in spirit and in truth.

- If you are looking for a book that offers a clear, and reproducible path for rapid church growth get this book.
- If you are looking for a book that has a biblical vision for church multiplication, get this book.
- If you are looking for a book that teaches how to make disciples that impact their piece of the world, get this book.

We have to stop thinking addition and think multiplication. This is just what Mike Napper did. We have to start believing that God can use us to plunder hell and populate heaven. We have a job to do. We are to go and make disciples of all nations, baptizing them in the name of the Father and of the Son and of the Holy Spirit, 20 and teaching them to obey everything Jesus has commanded us to obey.

That is what this book is all about. It's about a move of God. It's about being a part of something so great that only God gets the credit for it. It's about kicking down the gates of hell. It's about equipping people to do the work of ministry so that they might pass on what they know to the next generation.

The same Holy Spirit that sent tongues of fire on the disciples, the same Holy Spirit that gave courage to Peter and John when they were threatened to no longer speak in the name of Jesus, the same Holy Spirit that used Godly men and women to spread the message of Jesus over the known world is the same Holy Spirit that is in us today and through Him we can and will do exceedingly abundantly more than anything we have ever dreamed or imagined.

My prayer is that this book will reignite your passion and your vision for what God wants to do in and through you. That all of us would join hands and hearts and advance the kingdom of God. My prayer is that this book will inspire you with a renewed passion to join God's mission to plant churches, make disciples, and multiply God's kingdom to the ends of the earth.

There really is a heaven and there really is a hell and people really are going to one place or the other. If you are ready to do something about eternal realities, get this book.

Pastor Todd Cook
Senior Pastor of Sagebrush Community Church
Albuquerque, New Mexico

PREFACE

When I first felt the call to plant a church, I had more questions than answers. I wasn't sure where to begin, who would come with me, or how we would survive beyond the first few months. All I had was a burden in my heart, a fire in my bones, and a conviction that the Kingdom of God must advance.

That first church was planted with prayer, passion, and a lot of trial and error. But over time—by God's grace—we didn't just grow; we multiplied. One church became two. Two became three. Eventually, we saw a movement of churches, leaders, and disciples committed to multiplying the Kingdom, not just building a building.

This book was written for people like you—pastors, planters, pioneers, and dreamers—who feel called to reach more than one neighborhood, more than one generation, and more than one church.

I don't claim to have all the answers. I'm not offering a formula. What I offer is a roadmap shaped by Scripture, lived experience, and a relentless dependence on the Holy Spirit. You'll find here both the spiritual foundations and the practical strategies for starting and multiplying healthy churches.

This is not just about planting churches—it's about fulfilling the Great Commission in our generation. It's about raising up leaders, equipping disciples, and releasing people into the harvest.

My prayer is that this book will not only inspire you, but also equip you. May it serve as a companion on your church planting journey and help you multiply what God has entrusted to you.

Let's not just build churches. Let's multiply the Kingdom.
In Christ,

Mike Napper PhD

INTRODUCTION
The Vision for Church Planting

Church planting is not just a ministry strategy—it's a Kingdom mandate.

From the first gatherings of believers in Acts to the expanding networks of faith around the globe today, the Church has always been a movement, not just a meeting. It grows not by accident but by intentional obedience to Jesus' final words:

In this book, I'll share how I plant churches and disciple church planters. These are the practical strategies I've used throughout Africa to start new works, train pastors, and send missionaries. I believe these methods can be adapted and applied anywhere in the world—yes, even in your village or city.

That said, we are all different. We have unique personalities, backgrounds, and callings. So your approach may not look exactly like mine—and that's okay. Ministry is not one-size-fits-all. What matters most is that you're listening to the Holy Spirit and moving forward in obedience.

As I study Scripture, I see a wide range of leadership and ministry styles. Jesus often used what we now call humanitarian efforts—miracles of healing, feeding the hungry, and serving the broken—as a way to draw people to Himself. Paul charged ahead with boldness and authority, confronting opposition and planting churches in the hardest places. Barnabas led with encouragement and compassion, lifting others up when no one else would. Timothy was faithful, teachable, and willing to be shaped for leadership.

Each of these examples reveals something powerful: ministry must have both strength and love, boldness and humility. When you combine these characteristics in your leadership—when you pursue a Paul, become a Barnabas, and train a Timothy—you will build something with lasting substance. You'll fulfill the Great Commission with both strategy and heart.

Along the way, you'll need to make adjustments. Culture, language, and economics vary. Don't be discouraged if something doesn't work immediately. If it's not working, tweak it. Refine it.

Adapt it.

I've had people tell me flat-out, "That won't work here." But I'm convinced that almost anything can work—if you're willing to make the right modifications.

I once spoke with a missionary who had served in Europe for five years but had never planted a single church. When I asked why, he said, "The people are too hard to reach."
I gave him two thoughts.

First, maybe you're not called to reach those particular people. And if that's the case, it's okay to go find those who are open. Jesus hasn't stopped saving people—so let's go where the harvest is ripe.

Second, I asked, "Have you considered working with the poor or the refugees?" He quickly replied, "God didn't call me to work with them."

That answer grieved me. I believe if you begin your ministry by targeting the wealthy, you'll always struggle to reach and retain them. They are rarely looking for a Savior. But if you start with the poor—just as Jesus did—you'll find open hearts, build meaningful community, and establish a church that lasts. When you reach the poor, the wealthy often come later, not as those to be reached, but as partners to help. It's a win-win strategy for kingdom growth. Remember: strategies may shift, but the heart of the mission never does.

So lead like Paul with boldness. Love like Barnabas with compassion. And train your Timothys with patience and purpose. The future of the Church depends not just on what you build—but on who you equip.

Pastor Larry Maddox of Central Baptist Church in Katy, Texas, visited us in Togo, Africa, to witness firsthand this movement of God spreading across the continent. One night, as we celebrated new churches and the goodness of God, we had a conversation I'll never forget. Larry looked at me and said, "Mike, Jesus came to America on His way somewhere else." I don't know who first coined that phrase, but in that moment, it was exactly what I needed to hear. My passion has always been to take the gospel to the ends of the earth — and I believe that's the very heart of what the Apostle Paul envisioned as he penned the book of Acts.

Every new church is an act of obedience to that commission. Every church plant declares that the gospel still transforms lives, that people still need community, and that Jesus is still building His Church.

"Go therefore and make disciples of all nations, baptizing them in the name of the Father and of the Son and of the Holy Spirit, teaching them to observe all that I have commanded you. And behold, I am with you always, to the end of the age."
— Matthew 28:19–20, ESV

Here's the truth: church planting is hard. It will test your faith, your endurance, and your willingness to sacrifice. But it's not impossible. In fact, if you believe it is, you may need to reconsider your calling—because this work demands hard work, grace, and an unshakable belief that God can do the impossible through ordinary people.

It requires sacrifice, grit, vision, patience, and unwavering faith. It stretches you as a leader and deepens your dependence on God. It's spiritual warfare. It's relational ministry. And it's deeply personal.

But it's also one of the most powerful ways to expand the Kingdom of God on earth.

Studies consistently show that new churches are among the most effective ways to reach unchurched people, raise up new leaders, and serve diverse communities. Healthy church plants birth new disciples, impact neighborhoods, and become hubs of mission and multiplication.

This book exists to help you do exactly that—not just to plant one healthy church, but to multiply into six and beyond. Whether you're dreaming of your first church or already pastoring and praying about planting again, this book will help you:

- Clarify your calling
- Build a strong foundation
- Raise up a core team
- Develop systems that scale
- Launch with vision and confidence
- Multiply sustainably and spiritually

This is not just about growth—it's about reproduction. About building a sending culture. About equipping everyday people to do extraordinary things through the power of the Holy Spirit.

So what does it take to start six churches? It takes faith. It takes strategy. It takes the power of God and the faithfulness of His people.

What church planting doesn't require is years of over-planning, a flawless 12-step process, or waiting until the stars align and every leader is perfectly on board with a massive budget in place. Too often, I hear men say they've been "planning" for years—sitting in coffee shops, dreaming of the perfect launch while people outside those doors are dying without ever hearing the gospel.

Let me be clear: the world doesn't need more dreamers—it needs doers.

You don't need everything figured out. You don't need to wait until every detail is in place. Just go. Plant the church. Say yes to God. Work out the details as you move forward in faith.

Delay doesn't impress God—obedience does.

Are you ready?

Then let's begin.

CHAPTER 1

UNDERSTANDING THE MISSION FIELD

B efore you plant a church, you must plant yourself in the soil of understanding.

Church planting isn't about showing up with a clever strategy. Which unfortunately many try to do and fail. It's about stepping into a story God is already writing. So, it is more about listening to God and It's about listening to the heartbeat of a neighborhood, discerning the spiritual climate, and learning the language of a people who may have never heard the gospel in a way they could understand.

> *"When he saw the crowds, he had compassion for them, because they were harassed and helpless, like sheep without a shepherd."*
>
> *— Matthew 9:36, ESV*

That's where church planting begins—not with a plan, but with compassion.

Jesus was driven by compassion. Over and over in the Gospels, we see Him moved by the needs of people—not just physically, but spiritually and emotionally. "When He saw the crowds, He had compassion for them, because they were harassed and helpless, like sheep without a shepherd" (Matthew 9:36, ESV). His miracles weren't performed to impress—they were expressions of deep love. He touched lepers, wept with the grieving, fed the hungry, and welcomed the outcast. His compassion wasn't passive; it compelled Him to act. And that same compassion must drive us. If we're going to reach the lost and plant churches that reflect the heart of Christ, it starts with seeing people the way He did—with eyes of mercy and a heart that breaks for the broken.

1. See What Jesus Sees

Church planting can take different forms, and there's no single formula that fits every context. Some leaders choose to launch the first church themselves as the lead pastor, using a mother church model that later trains others to plant additional churches. Others start the first church, lead it for a few years, and then raise up a successor so they can move on to the next location. While these approaches can be effective, I've personally found them to be less aligned with the biblical model and often less fruitful in the long run.

The model I've followed—and continue to use—is to train pastors from the very beginning. From day one, they are equipped to lead their own churches, while I walk alongside them as a mentor, coach, and co-laborer. I believe this mirrors what Jesus did with the twelve apostles. He didn't do all the ministry Himself—He equipped others to do it and sent them out. The apostle Paul followed this same pattern, raising up leaders in every city and appointing elders to shepherd the churches he helped start.

At the end of the day, different methods can bear fruit if led by the Spirit. But one thing is certain: the only method that never works is doing nothing. Don't wait for the perfect plan. See what Jesus sees—the harvest is ready. Train leaders. Send them. Walk with them. And trust God to multiply His Church.

Jesus didn't just see statistics—He saw people. He didn't just notice brokenness—He moved toward it with compassion.

Far too often, church planting strategies are built around statistics, building size, and projected growth trends—focusing more on the expansion of facilities than the urgency of souls. Some plan a church plant not because they are burdened by the lost or moved by the call of God, but because a new development is going up across town or a demographic study suggests potential growth. But church planting should never be driven by spreadsheets alone. The real reason to plant a church is because people are dying without Jesus—right now. Hell is not waiting for your perfect launch date or capital campaign. We must be driven by compassion for the lost, not comfort in numbers. The call to plant churches is a call to rescue, to reach, and to respond to the heart of God for people who need salvation. Buildings don't transform lives—Jesus does.

Before you gather a launch team or design your first service, you must ask:

"What does Jesus see in this city? On this street? In these people?"

Church planting begins not with vision statements but with a burden from heaven.

2. Know the People, Not Just the Place

Understanding the mission field takes more than studying demographics. It requires presence. While charts, surveys, and population trends can provide useful information, they don't tell the whole story. Statistics can show you how many people live in an area, what language they speak, or what their average income is—but they can't show you the pain in a mother's eyes, the loneliness of a widow, or the hunger in a child's belly. They don't reveal spiritual emptiness, broken homes, or hearts crying out for hope.

To truly understand a mission field, you have to walk its streets, sit in its homes, eat its food, and listen to its people. You need to feel the rhythm of the community, hear the questions no survey can capture, and recognize the barriers no graph can explain. Presence builds trust. It opens doors. It reveals needs that are invisible from a distance.

Jesus didn't analyze the world from heaven—He stepped into it. "And the Word became flesh and dwelt among us" (John 1:14, ESV). He didn't study humanity from afar; He walked with people, touched the sick, and looked into the eyes of the broken. If we want to understand the mission field like Jesus did, we must be willing to show up—not just with plans, but with presence.

Start with the facts:
- Who lives here? (age, ethnicity, income, education)
- What languages are spoken?
- What is the dominant worldview? (Christian, agnostic, Muslim, etc.)
- What cultural rhythms shape the calendar and the community?

Then go deeper:
- What wounds does this neighborhood carry?
- What are the unspoken fears, hopes, and stories?
- What divides people here—and what could unite them?

Example:
A missionary in a village assumed poverty was the main issue. But after talking to residents, he discovered loneliness and isolation were far greater barriers to the gospel. That shaped his strategy: building small, intentional communities before focusing on large gatherings.

At our second church plant in Togo, Africa, something unforgettable happened. After several months of gathering, worshiping, and celebrating the birth of a new church, the village chief approached us. With deep sincerity in his voice, he said, "Thank you for bringing the true God to our people." He went on to say many have came in the past but never with God. His words carried weight—not just as a leader, but as a representative of the entire community. He continued, "Because of this, we are here. We want to worship and serve with you." It was a moment that reminded us: church planting isn't just about buildings or services—it's about transformation. When the Gospel reaches a village, it reaches hearts. And when leaders respond, entire communities can be changed.

3. Walk the Land and Pray

Before Joshua led Israel to take Jericho, he scouted it. Before Jesus preached in towns, He walked among them. Before the early church moved, they prayed.

Prayer walking is a powerful tool—but don't confuse it with casually strolling through a tourist destination, snapping selfies, and calling it a mission trip. True prayer walking is intentional and spiritual. It's about quietly interceding for the people, families, and strongholds in a community. It's walking the streets with open eyes and a burdened heart, asking God to move, to open doors, and to prepare hearts to receive the Gospel. It's not about being seen— it's about seeing what God sees.

- Discern spiritual strongholds
- Feel the heartbeat of the streets
- Hear from God in context
- See with heaven's eyes

Try walking or driving your city at different times of day. Pray: I find it helpful to visit the area on a Sunday morning during the hours of church to get a feel for the area.

- "Holy Spirit, what are You already doing here?"
- "What lies need to be broken?"
- "What hope can we restore?"
- "Who is spiritually hungry?"

Let prayer write your plan.

But I feel compelled to say: this shouldn't become a ten-year prayer followed by a twenty-year plan. There's nothing wrong with praying and planning — both are vital. But at some point, we have to move from talking about planting churches to actually planting them. The harvest is ready now. People need Jesus now. If we wait for the perfect moment, the perfect plan, or the perfect resources, we'll never start. Church planting requires faith, urgency, and obedience — not endless delays.

4. Honor the Past, Don't Ignore It

Church planting isn't spiritual colonization. You're not showing up to bring Jesus to a godless people—as if He hasn't already been there. You're stepping into a story that God has already begun writing. I often pause when I hear someone say they're "bringing Jesus back" to a city or region. The truth is, Jesus never left. He hasn't abandoned that place—the people may have drifted from Him, but He remains near. So rather than claiming to reintroduce God to the city, it's more accurate to say you're helping reintroduce the city to God. Church planting is about awakening hearts to the presence of Jesus that's already moving, already working, already waiting.

Meet with pastors/missionaries who've served the area for years.

Ask:
- "What's been tried before?"
- "What worked?"
- "What didn't?"

Honor their work—even if their style differs. Look for partnership, not competition.

"Let another praise you, and not your own mouth; a stranger, and not your own lips."

— Proverbs 27:2, ESV

Movements that multiply do so by walking in humility.

5. Study the Spiritual Climate

Every place has a spiritual atmosphere.

Is it:
- Apathetic?
- Religious but dry?
- Hungry but confused?

• Resistant from past spiritual wounds?

Ask God to reveal the kind of soil:
  • Hard-packed (skeptical, burned-out)
  • Rocky (shallow faith, fast burnout)
  • Thorny (distracted, consumer-driven)
  • Good (open, fertile)

It affects how you share Christ—with gentleness, relevance, and awareness of the local context. You're not showing up with a rehearsed script; you're listening, discerning, and responding to what the Spirit is already doing in people's hearts. It also changes how you build trust—slowly, through consistency, humility, and genuine care. You're not just preaching a message; you're embodying it through your presence. And finally, it reshapes how you recognize and measure fruit. Instead of only looking for large crowds or immediate decisions, you begin to notice the quieter signs of transformation—a returned conversation, a softened heart, a question asked in curiosity. These are seeds of the Kingdom. They may be small, but they matter. And they remind you that God is already at work long before the first service ever begins.

6. Clarify Your Calling with Conviction

Church planting is hard. Calling matters more than charisma. Always remember if it were easy, it would have already been done.

Ask:
  • Why here?
  • Why now?
  • Why me?

Get alone with God until you know. This clarity will sustain you when momentum stalls.

Fieldwork:
Write your calling story. What Scripture confirms it? What mentors have affirmed it? What inner burdens won't let you go?

Return to this often.

I get asked all the time how I knew I was supposed to be a missionary. Honestly, at 21 years old, missions wasn't even on the list of careers I was considering. It wasn't something I had planned—it was a desire that God placed deep in my heart. And that desire has remained strong for nearly three decades. Calling isn't always something you chase; sometimes, it's something that grabs hold of you—and never lets go.

7. Customize Strategy to the Mission Field

There's no one-size-fits-all model.

- Urban? You may need multiple services or marketplace outreach.
- Suburban? Family ministries might connect best.
- College town? Digital discipleship and flexible schedules.
- Rural? Trust and relational consistency are key.
- Village? Pack a lunch.

Your model should reflect your mission—not just your preferences. It's easy to design a church around what feels comfortable, familiar, or efficient to you as the leader. But church planting isn't about personal convenience—it's about aligning every part of your ministry with the purpose God has given you. That means your structure, your strategy, your style of leadership, even your service format, should all serve the mission first. Ask yourself: Does this model help us reach the lost? Does it empower discipleship? Does it reflect the heart of Jesus for this community? If the answer is no, then it may be time to adjust—not because your preferences are wrong, but because your mission is more important. The goal isn't to build something that fits you—it's to build something that fulfills the Great Commission.

8. Engage and Serve Before You Gather

Before you launch worship services, serve the city.

Ideals:
- Free community meals
- Volunteering in schools
- Hosting parenting workshops
- Cleaning up public spaces
- Partnering with nonprofits
- Host VBS style camps
- Showing of the Jesus films
- Rapid food relief

Serving builds trust. And trust is the currency of mission.

In any culture or community, people don't automatically open their hearts just because you show up with a Bible and a plan. They watch how you live long before they listen to what you say. Acts of genuine service—feeding the hungry, helping the sick, teaching a child, listening to a story—speak louder than sermons. When people see that you're not just there to preach at them but to walk with them, trust begins to grow.

And in missions, trust is everything. Without it, your message can be dismissed, your intentions misunderstood, and your influence limited. But when people trust you—when they believe you love them and aren't just using them as a project—they become open to the Gospel. Relationships are built. Conversations go deeper. Doors swing open.

Trust is the soil where seeds of truth take root. And the fastest, most lasting way to earn that trust is through humble, consistent service. It's not glamorous, but it's powerful. Because in serving others, you reflect the heart of Christ—"For even the Son of Man came not to be served but to serve, and to give his life as a ransom for many" (Mark 10:45, ESV).

If you want to plant a church that lasts, don't just preach—serve. Earn their trust. And then watch what God does with it.

9. Raise Up Local Leaders Early

You're not planting for people—you're planting with people.

Here's a confession: I'm dyslexic. One of the unfortunate side effects of dyslexia is difficulty with language learning. In fact, studies show that over 90% of people with dyslexia struggle to learn a foreign language—and I'm definitely one of them.

At first, I saw this as a major limitation. After all, how do you plant churches in a culture where you can't fluently speak the language? But in God's wisdom, what I thought was a weakness became one of the greatest strengths of our ministry. It forced me to rely on others—to raise up local leaders, to empower them, and to trust them with real responsibility from the beginning.

Instead of being the one doing all the speaking, leading, and preaching, I focused on training a few key leaders—people who could go further and speak more effectively than I ever could. And as they grew, they trained others. This simple but intentional approach led to the planting of multigenerational churches—churches led by the people, for the people, and deeply rooted in their own culture and community.

It turns out, my limitation wasn't a roadblock—it was a gift. It taught me that real multiplication doesn't happen when you try to do everything yourself. It happens when you plant with people, release them to lead, and trust God to do the rest.

Church planting is not a one-person show or a top-down project where you do all the work and others simply attend. If you see yourself as the sole builder and everyone else as spectators, you'll miss the heart of true multiplication—and you'll burn out quickly. The Church was never meant to be built on one leader's shoulders; it was always meant to be a body, a family, a team.

When you plant with people, you invite them into the mission from day one. You listen to their stories, recognize their gifts, and equip them to serve. You build ownership, not dependency. You raise up leaders, not just followers. People aren't just recipients of ministry—they become participants in it.

This approach fosters unity, growth, and long-term sustainability. It teaches the church to carry the mission together, so when challenges come—and they will—the church doesn't crumble because it was built on one person. It thrives because it was planted in shared faith, shared vision, and shared sacrifice.

Jesus didn't just preach to the crowds—He walked with His disciples. He taught them, empowered them, and then sent them. In the same way, church planting is not something you do for a community—it's something you do with them, so that together, you become the church God intended to plant.

Look for:
- People of peace (Luke 10)
- Spiritually curious seekers
- Influential locals
- Future disciples who can become leaders

Your future elders and deacons might be the ones greeting you at the market today or the ones you meet walking down a dirt road.

10. First 30-Day Field Plan

Weeks 1–2: Listening & Prayer
- Meet local leaders and pastors
- Prayer, walk neighborhoods and villages
- Attend community events

Weeks 3–4: Serve & Strategize
- Volunteer weekly at the same place
- Gather your core team for prayer
- Dream together about a church for this place
- Get to know the area well

Summary:
The Mission Field is Sacred Ground

You're not starting a project. You're stepping into a divine assignment.

This isn't just another ministry initiative, a checklist on your vision board, or a personal goal to achieve. Church planting is not a hobby or a side endeavor—it's a sacred calling. It's something God planned long before you ever said yes. When you plant a church, you're stepping into something far bigger than yourself. You're aligning your life with heaven's agenda for a specific place, at a specific time, for a specific people.

Projects have deadlines, budgets, and measurable outcomes—but divine assignments carry eternal impact. They demand prayer, perseverance, and total dependence on God. You don't get to control the results, but you are responsible for your obedience. And when you recognize that this is God's work—not just yours—it shifts everything. Your posture changes from managing a project to stewarding a mission. Your confidence no longer rests in your skill but in His calling.

This is holy ground. You're not just starting something new—you're continuing what God has already begun. You're stepping into His story, not writing your own. So treat it with reverence, move with boldness, and walk in faith—because the assignment is divine.

Love people before they love you. Walk the streets before you preach. Serve even if the city never serves you back.

When we first entered the village, we moved quickly. We had a team, a vision, and a clear sense that God was calling us to plant a church in this specific place. As soon as we arrived, we began looking for land to purchase—a base for ministry, a future home for worship, a place where the Gospel could take root.

But what we saw as progress, others saw as a threat.

There was a man who lived directly across the street from the land we were hoping to buy. He watched our every move with deep suspicion. One day, as we walked past his home, he stepped outside and called to us. His voice shook, and his eyes were wide with fear.

"Please," he said, "don't kill me."

We were stunned. This wasn't sarcasm. He was completely serious. In his eyes, our presence as foreigners—moving quickly, making inquiries, speaking in a different language—looked dangerous. He had no idea who we were or why we had come. And to him, we were not missionaries. We were outsiders, and possibly enemies.

That moment taught me something I'll never forget: trust doesn't come with your title. You may be a missionary, a pastor, or a church planter, but none of that matters to someone who doesn't know you. Some people have real fear when a stranger enters their village—especially a foreigner. You can't assume you're welcome just because your intentions are good.

So we stopped trying to push forward, and we started trying to love.

We greeted him each day. We learned his name. We brought small gifts. We asked about his family. We let him see us—not as strangers with a plan, but as people with compassion. Slowly, the fear in his eyes faded. He began to smile. He started asking questions—not about land, but about life. Over time, he became one of our greatest supporters. His home, once closed, became a place of hospitality.

And the land? We eventually purchased it—but only after earning the right to be trusted in the community. That village didn't just get a church building. It gained a family. And all of it began with love.

If you want to plant a church that lasts, don't start with land—start with hearts. Love always opens the door.

You're not the hero. Jesus is.

Reflection Questions:

- What are the top 3 needs of this community?
- Have I listened more than I've spoken?
- Who are 3 local leaders I can meet this month?
- How will I stay rooted in my calling during hard seasons?
- What does first-year success look like beyond attendance?

CHAPTER 2

BUILDING A TEAM

No one plants a church alone. God may give the vision to one person, but the fulfillment of that vision depends on a team of faithful, Spirit-filled believers.

Church planting is spiritual warfare. It's hard ground. You need a team not just to share the load, but to share the joy, prayer, sacrifice, growth, and miracle moments that happen when heaven touches earth.

> *"Two are better than one, because they have a good reward for their toil... And though a man might prevail against one who is alone, two will withstand him—a threefold cord is not quickly broken."*
>
> — Ecclesiastes 4:9, 12, ESV

You don't need a large team to start. You need the right people with the right heart in the right order.

This was never meant to be a one-person show. Kingdom ministry is team ministry. I'm often asked if I believe teams from the U.S. truly benefit the missionary and the mission field. The answer is yes — without a doubt. I host over 20 teams a year, and every single one plays a vital role in helping us plant the next church. But I also want to offer a word of caution: choose your teams wisely. Some of my hardest days as a missionary have come because I allowed the wrong team to come and work alongside us. The right team is a blessing. The wrong team can create challenges you never expected.

1. The Power of Team in the Early Church

In Acts, Jesus sent them two by two (Mark 6:7). Paul never planted alone—he had Barnabas, Timothy, Silas, Luke. The early Church multiplied because teams multiplied, not just individuals.

> Alan Hirsch, The Forgotten Ways (Grand Rapids: Brazos Press, 2006), 34.
> — Hirsch calls for a return to the dynamics of the early church for multiplication.

To my missionary friends; While partnering with other American missionaries can seem like a natural and convenient choice, it often comes with hidden dangers. Statistically, partnerships between foreign missionaries—especially those from the same culture—can lead to competition, comparison, vision drift, or even fractured relationships due to differing philosophies of ministry or personality clashes. When two Americans try to lead side by side in a foreign context, cultural blind spots can be amplified rather than balanced. In contrast, when you intentionally invest in national pastors, training and discipling them to lead their own people, you multiply your effectiveness and honor the indigenous leadership God is already raising up. Empowering nationals ensures long-term sustainability and cultural relevance, while keeping the mission focused on the people—not the preferences of outsiders. Healthy collaboration is possible, but it must be rooted in humility, clarity of purpose, and a willingness to step back and let others lead.

Teaching Point:
Conflict with Other Missionaries Is the #1 Reason Americans Leave the Field.
It may surprise you, but the leading cause of missionary

resignation isn't culture shock, financial stress, or persecution—it's conflict with other missionaries. Studies, including those from the Missionary Attrition Project, have consistently shown that interpersonal tension among fellow missionaries—especially those from the same country—is the most common reason for early departure from the field.

Why? When multiple strong personalities, differing visions, and cultural expectations collide without clear communication or shared humility, division often follows. American missionaries, in particular, may struggle with collaboration when roles are not clearly defined or when personal agendas override kingdom unity.

This is why it's critical to cultivate emotional maturity, humility, and a shared, Spirit-led vision in any team. But even more importantly, prioritizing the training and empowering of national leaders often proves to be more fruitful and sustainable. Indigenous pastors are rooted in the culture, language, and community. When we disciple and release them, we avoid many of the conflicts that come with foreign partnerships—and we follow the biblical pattern of multiplication through local leadership.

In short:
Unity is mission-critical, and pride is mission-ending.
Kingdom ministry is team ministry.

2. Who You Build With Matters More Than How Many

It can be tempting to gather a crowd, but don't rush to build a big team. Build a strong one.

Look for people who are:
- Spiritually mature
- Willing to serve, not just lead
- Emotionally healthy and teachable
- Loyal to the vision, not just the leader
- Committed to the mission, not their position

It's better to launch with five sold-out disciples than with twenty-five undecided spectators.

Why? Because movements are never built on crowds—they're built on commitment. A small group of people who are fully surrendered to the mission, who love Jesus deeply, and who are willing to serve, sacrifice, and multiply themselves will always go farther than a room full of people who are just curious or casually attending.

Spectators consume; disciples contribute. Spectators wait to be served; disciples step up to serve others. Spectators are impressed by what's happening; disciples are invested in what God is doing. When you launch with people who are truly "all in," you're laying a foundation that can carry the weight of future growth. You're planting a church that doesn't just gather people but makes disciples who make disciples.

Jesus Himself started with twelve. And among them, it was the few who were truly faithful that turned the world upside down. So don't measure your launch by numbers alone. Look for faith, hunger, and obedience. Five sold-out disciples who pray, serve, give, and lead will always be more powerful than a passive crowd. Start with the committed—and watch how God multiplies the rest.

3. Pray Your Team Into Place

Team building isn't just a leadership exercise—it's a spiritual practice. (CHAT about how the right team can kill the church or launch it)

When you're planting a church, assembling a team isn't like staffing a business or organizing a volunteer roster. It's a deeply spiritual process that requires prayer, discernment, and dependence on the Holy Spirit. You're not just looking for people with skills—you're looking for people with surrendered hearts. The goal isn't to gather talent for a task; it's to cultivate unity around a Kingdom calling.

In my experience, building a team starts long before people get titles or responsibilities. It begins with prayerfully discerning who God is already raising up. I've learned to look past charisma and focus on character. I ask, "Is this person teachable? Faithful? Spirit-led? Will they still show up when it's hard and no one is clapping?" Those are the people who last. Those are the people who multiply.

I've also come to realize that team chemistry isn't accidental—it's cultivated through shared values, open communication, and a mutual commitment to the mission. When a team prays together, serves together, and sacrifices together, they don't just work well together—they grow spiritually, forming a bond that the enemy has a hard time breaking.

Remember: Jesus didn't just recruit a team—He formed one. He spent time with them, challenged them, corrected them, and sent them out empowered. If Jesus treated team building as a spiritual priority, we must too. Because the strength of your team will often determine the strength—and the sustainability—of your church plant.

In two of our church plant locations, we witnessed firsthand how God goes ahead of us—even when we don't have all the information. In both cases, we placed pastors in villages where we felt led to plant, unaware that many people there spoke a different tribal language than the one we had anticipated. It wasn't until later, after the churches were already taking root, that we discovered something remarkable: the pastors we had assigned just so happened to speak the exact tribal language of those communities. We hadn't planned it that way—but God had. What we thought was a practical decision turned out to be divine placement. It was a powerful reminder that the Holy Spirit is always orchestrating details we can't see, aligning leaders with communities, and preparing the soil long before we ever arrive.

Ask God to show you:
- Who He is sending
- Who you should invite
- Who is not called to this assignment (even if they're talented)

Ask intercessors to pray with you over potential team members. Let the Holy Spirit do the choosing.

4. Define Roles Early—Keep Them Flexible

Clarity brings unity. Even early on, people want to know: What am I responsible for? Who do I report to? What does success look like? Without clear answers, even the most committed leaders can end up working against each other. I saw this firsthand in one of our early church plants. We had placed two strong leaders in the same location—both gifted, both passionate about the mission. The problem? I hadn't clearly defined who was actually leading. Within a few weeks, both men believed they were the pastor. Each one was making decisions, casting vision, and trying to lead the people in different directions. What started as a promising launch quickly turned into quiet confusion and tension among the team and the congregation.

Once I realized what was happening, we sat down, clarified roles, and affirmed one of them as the lead pastor while inviting the other into a key supporting leadership role. From that point forward, things changed. The team aligned, the church began to grow, and the people had a clear shepherd to follow. That experience taught me that spiritual gifting alone isn't enough—structure and clarity are essential. When everyone knows their role and respects the leadership God has put in place, unity flourishes and the mission moves forward with strength.

Common roles:
- Worship leader — Cultivates a culture of praise
- Kids coordinator — Designs safe, engaging ministry
- Hospitality leader — Oversees setup, greeting, follow-up
- Prayer leader — Covers the team in intercession
- Outreach leader — Mobilizes evangelism and service
- Administrator — Manages finances and communication

Early on, people may wear many hats — that's okay. Just be clear.

Every church planter knows this: when you're just getting started, everyone does everything. The pastor is also the janitor, the worship leader, the small group coordinator, the youth mentor, and sometimes even the one digging the foundation. Volunteers double as greeters, Sunday school teachers, and security. And the guy who just got saved last month might be setting up the sound system this month.

This is the reality of a new work — and it's beautiful.

But while roles may overlap, the vision must stay clear.

Clarity is what keeps momentum alive when structure is still forming. People are more willing to sacrifice and serve when they understand what they're building. They're not just doing a job — they're laying a foundation for a future movement.

So yes — wear multiple hats.

Lead worship, sweep the floors, drive the van, print the flyers, teach the kids.

But never stop saying: "We are planting a church that will plant more churches."

That mindset is what separates struggling ministries from multiplying ones.

And here's the truth: even in our most remote churches — we have this mindset.

We don't wait for comfort or convenience to embrace the call.

We don't wait until we have a full staff or a budget line for every ministry.

We work with what we have — and we work with purpose.

In the village churches we've planted, people still wear many hats. The pastor may also be the local schoolteacher. The worship leader may also be hauling water from the well. The elders may be farming all week, but preaching on Sunday. But in the midst of it all, there is clarity of mission — we are here to multiply.

We don't just gather — we prepare to go.
We don't just survive — we strategize.
We don't just fill a building — we fill a calling.

Even in humble beginnings, we speak with sending language.
Even when there's only one church, we talk about the second.
Even with limited hands, we train more hands.

So yes — early on, we wear many hats.
But we wear them with purpose, direction, and vision.
Because we know: this isn't just a church. This is the beginning of a movement.

And even in the remote village church — we have this.

5. Create a Core Team Covenant

Healthy teams are built on shared expectations and shared sacrifice.

Healthy teams are built on shared expectations and shared sacrifice—not on one person sitting on the throne. One of the greatest dangers in church planting is when a team begins to revolve around a single strong personality. Whether intentional or not, it's easy for one leader to start making all the decisions, casting all the vision, and carrying all the weight—until they begin to function more like a king than a servant. But the Church already has a King—and it's not any of us. It's Jesus.

When teams lose sight of that, dysfunction sets in. Pride grows, control tightens, and trust erodes. But when expectations are shared, when responsibilities are distributed, and when every team member sacrifices for the good of the mission, something powerful happens: the church reflects the heart of Christ. There's unity, humility, and clarity of purpose.

I've seen this firsthand. When leadership is submitted to Christ and shared among the team, people flourish. Gifts emerge. Burdens are carried together. And best of all, no one gets the glory but Jesus. Because healthy teams don't need a king—they need the King. Let Jesus lead, and let every team member play their part with joy and humility. That's the kind of leadership that lasts.

Agree on:
- Time commitments
- Financial giving expectations
- Prayer rhythms
- Conflict resolution practices
- Commitment to outreach

This isn't legalism. It protects the vision and unites the team.

We had this issue early on with a new pastor who, unfortunately, began to see himself more as a king than a servant leader. At first, things seemed promising. He was passionate, articulate, and knew the local language well. But as the church began to grow and he gained influence, a dangerous shift started to take place. Instead of pointing people to Jesus, he began drawing people to himself. Decisions became controlling. Correction turned into intimidation. Eventually, he started mistreating members of the congregation and other leaders under him.

It escalated to the point where he began threatening individuals with physical harm—and even made threats of death. What began as a church plant rooted in love, humility, and service was quickly becoming a place of fear and spiritual manipulation. We had to intervene and remove him from leadership, but the damage was already done. Trust had been broken, and healing took time.

This experience taught me a hard but necessary lesson: in some cultures, especially in parts of Africa where leadership can be closely tied to power and dominance, a missionary church planter must be extremely discerning when appointing pastors. If you place the wrong person in charge—someone who sees the church as a throne rather than a platform to serve—you don't just risk losing influence; you risk harming people spiritually, emotionally, and even physically.

Cultural context matters. In some regions, the role of a "pastor" is viewed with the same reverence and authority as a chief or tribal leader. If that authority is abused, it can create a toxic environment that's hard to recover from. That's why character must always outweigh charisma when choosing leaders. And it's also why shared leadership and mutual accountability are so vital. We're not building empires—we're building the Kingdom. And in the Kingdom of God, there's only one King—Jesus.

We must train, empower, and trust leaders—but we must also remain vigilant. Appoint slowly. Watch closely. And always build structures that prevent one man from claiming a crown that doesn't belong to him.

6. Prioritize Relationship Over Skill

Your team is not a ministry machine—it's a family. You need to trust the people beside you.

Foster relationships by:
- Eating together (My favorite memory is eating goat while watching the Jesus films with local pastors)
- Sharing testimonies and prayer
- Taking retreats or off-site planning days
- Studying the Word together
- Laughing and having fun — joy fuels mission

One of our favorite traditions in ministry is something simple, but deeply meaningful—we host a barbecue at our home. When our USA mission teams come to serve alongside us, we always carve out time to gather with them and our African pastors, leaders, and church members around the grill. We don't just do it for the food (though the grilled chicken and homemade sides are always a hit)—we do it for the relationships. In a setting that's casual and joyful, walls come down. Conversations flow. Laughter fills the air. We share testimonies, talk about life and ministry, and learn from one another. It's in these moments—over shared meals and smoky grills—that something powerful happens: we become more than ministry partners; we become family. The barbecue becomes more than a meal—it's a place where cultures collide and unity is forged. It deepens our commitment to one another and reminds us why we do what we do: not just to build churches, but to build people, together.

Don't let task lists replace friendship and spiritual unity.

In the fast pace of church planting and missions, it's easy to become consumed by logistics—schedules, meetings, deadlines, and to-do lists. The mission is urgent, and there's always something that needs to be done. But if we're not careful, we can start operating more like a business team than a spiritual family. We begin prioritizing productivity over people. And when that happens, we lose something essential.

Ministry doesn't just run on efficiency—it runs on relationship. The early church didn't change the world because they had perfect planning software or flawless systems. They changed the world because they were devoted to one another, to prayer, to breaking bread, and to the Spirit's leading (Acts 2:42). They were united in heart and purpose.

I've learned that if I'm not intentional, I can treat my team like coworkers instead of brothers and sisters. That's why we create space for meals, conversations, and prayer—not just planning sessions. We slow down to ask how someone's really doing, not just what they're doing. Because spiritual unity isn't built through task lists—it's built through time, transparency, and shared faith.

So yes, build structure. Stay organized. Keep the mission moving. But don't let the mission become mechanical. Protect the friendships. Guard the unity. Because a team that prays together, eats together, laughs together, and loves one another deeply will always go further than one that's simply checking off tasks.

7. Deal with Conflict Early and Biblically

Planting doesn't create conflict—it reveals it.

One of the things I've learned through years of church planting is that launching a new work doesn't necessarily cause problems—it simply brings existing ones to the surface. When you step out to plant a church, the pressure, uncertainty, and spiritual warfare have a way of exposing what's already in people's hearts. Hidden pride, unresolved tension, competing visions, and unmet expectations all tend to rise when the work gets real. That's not something to fear—it's something to expect.

Early on, I used to be surprised when conflict showed up during the planting process. I thought maybe I'd made a mistake or chosen the wrong people. But over time, I came to realize that planting doesn't create conflict—it just shines a light on it. And in God's mercy, that exposure is an opportunity for growth. It gives you the chance to address issues before they take root and poison the foundation of the church. It forces honest conversations, clarifies motives, and deepens trust among your core team—if you respond with humility and grace.

So don't run from conflict when it comes. Use it. Let it refine your team and shape your culture. A church built on fake unity won't stand. But a church that works through real tension with love and truth becomes strong and resilient. Conflict isn't the enemy—division is. And the only way to guard against division is to let the light in early.

You'll face:
- Personality clashes
- Misunderstood expectations
- Old church wounds
- Misaligned priorities

Don't avoid conflict. Resolve it biblically.

Teach:
Matthew chapter 18 principles

Matthew 18 is one of the most important chapters in the Bible when it comes to Kingdom relationships, leadership, and church culture. It's like a relational blueprint for how the Body of Christ should operate. Here are the key principles found in Matthew 18:

1. Humility is the foundation of greatness (Matthew 18:1–4)
Jesus teaches that the greatest in the Kingdom is the one who humbles himself like a child. Kingdom leadership isn't about power or platform—it's about dependence on God, teachability, and a humble heart.

2. Protect the vulnerable and avoid causing others to stumble (Matthew 18:5–7)
Jesus gives a serious warning about causing "little ones" who believe in Him to stumble. Leaders must be cautious not to use their position, influence, or actions to harm or mislead others. There is a high level of accountability in the Kingdom.

3. Deal radically with sin in your own life (Matthew 18:8–9)
We're told to cut off anything in our lives that causes us to sin. It's about personal holiness and taking sin seriously—for our sake and the sake of others who follow us.

4. Value the one—the lost and overlooked matter to God (Matthew 18:10–14)
Jesus tells the parable of the lost sheep to emphasize that God pursues the one who strays. In Kingdom leadership, no person is expendable. Every person matters.

5. Confront sin with grace and clarity (Matthew 18:15–17)
Jesus gives us a clear model for dealing with conflict and sin within the church:

- First, go to the person privately.
- If they don't listen, bring one or two others.
- If they still refuse to repent, bring it to the church.
- If they still reject correction, treat them as an outsider—but always with a redemptive heart.

This protects the unity of the church and promotes reconciliation over gossip or division.

6. The power of agreement in prayer and spiritual authority (Matthew 18:18–20)
Jesus teaches that what is bound or loosed on earth has spiritual impact. He also reminds us that where two or three gather in His name, He is present. Unity and agreement in prayer are powerful Kingdom dynamics.

7. Forgiveness is not optional—it's unlimited (Matthew 18:21–35)
Peter asks how many times he should forgive—Jesus answers not seven times, but seventy-seven times. Then He shares the parable of the unforgiving servant to illustrate how serious God is about forgiveness. We forgive because we have been forgiven.

Summary:
The Matthew 18 principles shape the heart of Kingdom leadership:

- Be humble.
- Guard the vulnerable.
- Take personal sin seriously.
- Pursue the lost.
- Handle conflict biblically.
- Agree in unity and prayer.
- Forgive without limit.

A healthy team isn't friction-free. It knows how to fight fair and forgive fast.

experienced this firsthand with one of the pastors we had brought into our church planting network. On the surface, everything looked promising. He was passionate, had strong leadership qualities, and spoke the local language. But as the ministry began to grow, so did underlying tension. He began pushing his own agenda, making decisions without accountability, and slowly distancing himself from the core values that held our team together. At first, I questioned myself. Had I made a bad leadership choice? Was this conflict something I needed to confront head-on?

But instead of reacting with anger or trying to force him out, I responded with love, grace, and a clear commitment to the mission God had given us. I kept the lines of communication open, reinforced the vision, and prayed daily for God to either bring unity—or to bring clarity. And then, without me having to take any drastic measures, God did exactly that.

The pastor removed himself from our ministry.

It wasn't through a fight or a dramatic split. It was peaceful. And because it wasn't fueled by flesh but guided by the Spirit, we were spared legal issues, broken relationships, and future division in the team. Looking back, I know that if I had forced the situation, we would have lost more than just a pastor—we could have lost credibility, trust, and momentum.

That experience taught me that conflict in church planting is inevitable—but it's also revealing. And when handled with love and a commitment to the calling, God has a way of resolving things in ways we never could. The goal isn't to avoid conflict, but to face it with spiritual maturity—knowing that God often uses it to protect the integrity of the mission.

8. Multiplication Begins with the Core

If your team only exists to support you, growth will stall. But if your team multiplies disciples, growth happens naturally.

Build a culture of:
- Training replacements
- Inviting others into leadership
- Reproducing small groups
- Celebrating multiplication over accumulation

Every team member is a planter-in-training.

9. Stories from the Field

Story 1:

I remember a church planter in America who set out with high hopes. He had a small team, a storefront location, some financial support, and the passion to launch a new church. On paper, it looked like everything was in place. But after a little over a year, they closed the doors for good. Why? It wasn't for lack of space or resources—it was because the heart of the team wasn't right.

I spoke with one of his team members who shared something that stuck with me. Instead of focusing on the mission, they spent their time visiting other churches just to criticize what others were doing. They would leave saying things like, "We're not going to do that," as if tearing others down was part of casting vision. But negativity doesn't build churches. Pride doesn't win souls.

The team had a building, but not a burden. They had ideas, but not unity. They were focused on methods—not the mission.

When choosing your church planting team, don't just look for talent—look for attitude. Surround yourself with people who are passionate about reaching the lost, not just perfecting organizational style. You need team members who speak life, stay humble, and believe in the power of the Gospel—not those who measure success by comparison. Church planting is too hard to carry dead weight in the form of critical spirits. Build with people who lift up the mission and each other. That's how churches take root—and stay rooted.

Story 2:

Years ago, a young pastor arrived in Charlotte, North Carolina with little more than a Bible in his hand, a fire in his heart, and a dream to plant a healthy, gospel-centered church. He didn't have a large launch team, a ministry degree from a prestigious seminary, or a master plan—just a clear calling from God and a deep burden for the city. He began small, meeting with a handful of families, preaching faithfully, praying earnestly, and serving the community with quiet consistency. The early years were slow, marked more by grit than glamour. But he stayed the course. He discipled people. He trained leaders. He didn't chase trends—he built on truth. Now, more than 50 years later, that church is thriving. It runs nearly 1,500 people, has birthed ministries, supported missionaries, and continues to be a lighthouse in the city. What started as a dream became a legacy—not because of quick success, but because of steady obedience. His story is a reminder that church planting isn't just about what you build in the first five years—it's about what still stands in 50.

Story 3:
Once I knew a Missionary who kept inviting American teams to move to Africa with the goal of building the perfect church. His plan was to wait until he had assembled the perfect team before launching. I remember asking him "when do you think you'll be ready to start the church" His answer was "When I have the perfect American team" within two years he had resigned from the mission field because that perfect team never came.

10 Questions to Ask as You Build

- Who are the 3 people I trust most to pray and dream with me?
- Who shows humility, hunger, and heart for people—not just skill?
- What roles are essential right now?
- How will I care for my team emotionally and spiritually?
- Am I building leaders or just helpers?

Steve Addison, Movements That Change the World (Downers Grove: IVP, 2011), 43. — Addison identifies essential characteristics of world-changing movements.

Summary:
Start With the Right People

Every move of God begins with people who say "yes." Before there's a crowd, there's a core. That core is your first church.

Treat them with honor, love, and intentionality.

> *"One who is faithful in a very little is also faithful in much…"*
>
> — Luke 16:10, ESV

Field Assignment
- Write a 1-page team vision statement and review it regularly.
- Draft a Core Team Covenant and review it with your top 3 leaders.
- Spend one day this week praying by name for current or potential team members.

CHAPTER 3

SECURING RESOURCES

Church planting takes more than passion — it takes provision.

Passion is essential. It's what gets you moving when no one else believes in the vision. It fuels the late nights, the long prayers, and the tireless work of breaking new ground. But passion alone isn't enough. You can be full of vision and still burn out if there's no provision to sustain the mission.

Provision isn't just about money—though financial support matters. It's also about people, resources, timing, and spiritual covering. You need faithful partners who will serve, give, and pray. You need places to meet, tools to teach, and leaders to multiply. And most importantly, you need God's hand guiding each step.

I've planted churches with very little—sometimes with no clear funding and only a few committed people—but every time, God provided what was needed as we moved forward in obedience. Provision doesn't always come before you start. Often, it meets you on the road. The key is to trust that if God truly called you, He will also equip you.

So yes, have passion. Dream big. Pray bold prayers. But also look for God's provision—because when calling and provision meet, that's where church planting moves from surviving to thriving. Passion ignites the vision, but provision sustains the mission.

God is your provider. But He calls you to plan wisely, ask boldly, and steward faithfully. Resources aren't the goal of ministry, but they are tools that empower the mission. You need them not to build comfort, but to reach people, make disciples, and multiply leaders.

> *"For which of you, desiring to build a tower, does not first sit down and count the cost, whether he has enough to complete it?"*
>
> — Luke 14:28, ESV

Faith and planning aren't enemies — they're partners in obedience.

1. What Do You Actually Need?

Before you fundraise or buy equipment, ask:
"What does this church require to launch well?"

Break it down:
1. People resources
   • Core team and volunteers
   • Coaches and mentors
   • Prayer partners
   • Launch team (setup, worship, kids, hospitality, tech)

My plan for launching a church looks very different depending on the context—whether I'm planting a first-generation church or launching a new church as an extension of an existing one.

When I'm planting a first church in a new area—where there is no previous congregation, no leadership infrastructure, and often no Christian presence—the approach is foundational. Everything starts from scratch. It's about pioneering, earning trust in the community, identifying local leaders, and building slowly with strong relational roots. In those cases, I focus heavily on prayer walking, connecting with the community, identifying a person of peace, and training a pastor from the ground up. I have to think long-term, knowing that the early stages may be small and slow, but necessary to establish lasting spiritual impact.

On the other hand, when I plant a church from an existing one—what some might call a daughter church—I already have a base of support. There's usually a sending church, trained leaders, and often some resources or people already prepared to go. In that case, the focus shifts. It's more about momentum than foundation-building. I'm replicating culture, extending vision, and deploying leaders who've already been discipled and equipped. The structure is stronger, the strategy more focused, and the timeline often quicker because the groundwork has already been laid.

Both types of church plants are valuable—and necessary—but they require different strategies, expectations, and timelines. One is pioneering; the other is multiplying. Both require faith, leadership, and flexibility. As a planter, your role is to recognize what kind of planting you're doing and adjust your plan accordingly—because planting isn't a one-size-fits-all mission. It's about listening to God, knowing the soil, and planting in a way that allows the roots to grow deep and the fruit to last.

2. Financial resources
- Pre-launch budget (equipment, marketing, outreach)
- Monthly budget (rent, supplies, staff)
- Emergency reserves
- Giving system (online, mobile, envelopes)

3. Physical resources
- Sound equipment
- Kids ministry supplies
- Hospitality items (signage, coffee, tables)
- Venue
- Admin/office space

Tip:
In the early stages of church planting, it's easy to feel pressure to look the part — to buy the best sound system, print professional banners, get matching T-shirts, and create a social media presence that rivals megachurches. But here's the truth: impressive optics

don't produce lasting fruit.

I've built some amazing churches with nothing more than a three-dollar soccer ball.

That's right. In some places, a soccer ball did more for evangelism than an LED screen ever could. It drew kids. The kids brought their parents. The parents heard the gospel. One ball, some joy, and the power of the Spirit — and suddenly, a church was born.

Meanwhile, I've also seen people spend massive amounts of money on dead-end ideas — flashy launches, expensive equipment, marketing campaigns — with no real return. Because money can't replace mission. And no budget can substitute for boldness, obedience, and love for people.

Here's what I've learned:

In the early days, spend less on appearance and more on impact.

- Invest in discipleship materials, not decorations.
- Prioritize transportation to reach the unreached, not stage lights to impress the reached.
- Focus on training leaders, not polishing your logo.
- Use tools that build relationships, not just platforms.

If all you have is a Bible, a soccer ball, and a willing heart — you can plant a church. I've seen it happen. I've done it.

That's not to say quality doesn't matter — but quality without mission is just noise.

And money without movement is just waste.

Early on, your best investments are time, people, and presence.

It's sitting in homes. Walking dirt roads. Teaching the Word. Praying with the sick. Feeding the hungry. Loving the forgotten. Multiplying leaders. Training the faithful.

So be wise. Steward well.

You don't need everything — you just need the right things.

Don't overspend trying to look successful.

Focus on what multiplies.

Because when you build with the right materials —

even a $3 soccer ball can shake a village, and spark a movement.

2. Where Does Provision Come From?

Provision usually comes from multiple streams:

Personal supporters

Personal supporters have played a vital role in helping us build more than just churches—they've helped us build foundations for entire communities. While preaching, training, and discipling are at the heart of the mission, physical structures are often necessary for long-term impact. Whether it's a simple shelter for worship, a training center for pastors, or a school building for children, these projects require resources we can't generate alone. Our personal supporters—those who believe in the vision and invest sacrificially—have been the bridge between the calling and the construction. They may not be in the field with us, but they are building alongside us with every gift they give. Their generosity has helped turn vision into reality, faith into something tangible, and temporary gatherings into permanent Gospel outposts. Without them, many of the churches and ministries we've planted would still be waiting for walls.

• Friends, family, former church connections

Our ability to build physical church structures has been made possible through the generosity of personal supporters—friends, family members, and connections from former churches who believe in the mission God has called us to. While we're on the ground planting churches and training pastors, these faithful partners are standing behind us, helping turn vision into reality. Their support has allowed us to construct buildings where believers can gather, where communities can find hope, and where future leaders can be trained. These aren't just donations—they're bricks of obedience, generosity, and eternal investment. Every wall raised and roof completed is a testimony to the power of partnership in the Kingdom of God. We may be the ones placing pastors and preaching the Gospel, but it's our supporters who help build the places where the Gospel will take root for generations to come.

Church partnerships
- One-time gifts (A must)
- Monthly support (Got to have it)
- Donated equipment (Please)
- People sent to help (all of our church plants start this way)

Church partnerships are key to sustainable and multiplying ministry. While personal supporters are vital, partnerships with churches—both in the U.S. and abroad—have been a cornerstone of our ability to plant, build, and train at a greater scale. These churches aren't just financial sponsors; they're co-laborers in the mission. Through their prayers, giving, and sometimes sending teams, we've been able to plant churches, construct buildings, equip pastors, and impact entire villages. A healthy church partnering with a missionary or church planter is a picture of the body of Christ in action—each part doing its role to fulfill the Great Commission. I've seen firsthand how one church's obedience can ignite a movement on the other side of the world. When local churches partner globally, something powerful happens: the Kingdom grows faster, stronger, and deeper. No one plants alone—and we're grateful to be in this mission together.

Tip:
Build relationships before you ask. Focus on Kingdom partnership.

One of the most important lessons I've learned in missions and church planting is this: never lead with a request—lead with a relationship. People want to know your heart before they hear your need. Before you talk about money, buildings, or projects, take the time to build trust. Share your story. Listen to theirs. Pray together. Celebrate what God is doing on both sides of the partnership.

When your goal is true Kingdom partnership—not just financial support—you'll find that people are far more willing to walk alongside you. I've sat with pastors, friends, and former church members over coffee, not to present a pitch, but to share a vision. Many of those conversations turned into long-term partnerships that helped us plant churches, train pastors, and build lasting Gospel impact. But the trust had to come first.

Kingdom partnerships are built on mutual respect, shared vision, and the understanding that we're better together. When you focus on relationships, the support will come—not because you pressured someone, but because they believe in what God is doing through you. And when people feel like partners, not just donors, they stay committed for the long haul. So, take your time. Build the relationship. Let the ask come from a place of unity, not urgency. That's where real partnership begins.

Denominations/networks
- Grants, matching funds (This has been key)
- Coaching and accountability (Some are not familiar with giving; so coach them.)
- Training and legal support

Your core team
- Teach generosity early. Your team should be first to give — in time and finances.

One of the most humbling things I've witnessed in ministry is the generosity of local pastors and leaders in Africa. Long before outside support arrives, they are often the first to give—and sometimes, they give everything they have. I've seen pastors bring the first fruits of their gardens, walk miles to attend training, or sell what little they own just to buy materials for a church gathering. They don't wait until conditions are ideal; they give because they believe. Their faith isn't built on abundance—it's built on obedience. And their sacrifice speaks louder than any sermon. It challenges me deeply, because while others may give from their excess, these leaders give from their lack, trusting that God will provide. Their example reminds me that true ministry begins not with resources, but with a willing heart. They are not just recipients of the mission—they are leaders of it, walking by faith and building the Kingdom one sacrifice at a time.

3. Fundraising is Discipleship

Asking for money makes leaders nervous. But you're not asking for yourself — you're inviting people to invest in eternity.

Note:
Don't be the pastor who invites missionaries or church planters to your church just to preach another sermon. They're not coming to replace your pulpit—they're coming to report on the miracles. Give them space to tell the God-sized stories—the kind that stir faith, break hearts, and move people to action. Stories of villages being reached, pastors being raised up, churches being planted in unreached areas, and lives being transformed by the Gospel. These testimonies aren't just updates—they're fuel for the Church. They remind people that the Great Commission is still active, that God is still moving, and that we all have a part to play. When a missionary comes, don't just give them the pulpit—give them the freedom to testify. That moment might be the spark that ignites the next wave of senders, givers, or goers in your church.

Approach fundraising as:
- Vision casting — tell stories, show impact.
- Discipleship — generosity grows people.
- Obedience — invite people to invest where God is moving.

> *"Each one must give as he has decided in his heart, not reluctantly or under compulsion, for God loves a cheerful giver."*
>
> — 2 Corinthians 9:7, ESV

Be transparent. Be grateful. Be bold.
These three qualities have guided me through countless conversations with churches, supporters, and ministry partners. First, be transparent. Don't sugarcoat the challenges. Share the real needs, the spiritual battles, and the honest condition of the field. People don't connect with polished perfection—they connect with authenticity. When you're honest about the highs and lows, your partners feel trusted and invited into the journey, not just the highlight reel.

Second, be grateful. Never take a single prayer, dollar, or word of encouragement for granted. Express your thanks often and sincerely. I've found that people are more willing to continue investing when they know their support is not just helping but truly valued. Gratitude builds trust and deepens relationships. Let your supporters know they are part of something eternal—and that you couldn't do it without them.

Finally, be bold. Don't be afraid to cast big vision, to share God-sized dreams that go beyond your current reality. People are inspired by faith. When you speak boldly about what God has called you to do, you give others the opportunity to step into that vision with you. Boldness isn't arrogance—it's confidence that God will provide and do what only He can do.

So as you build relationships and raise support, remember: Be transparent enough to be real, grateful enough to be trusted, and bold enough to move mountains. So, don't ask for $5000.00 when you need $50,0000. Ask for the $50,0000 and watch how God lands it.

4. Build a Clear, Credible Budget To Match the Vision

People won't give to fog. Create a simple, realistic budget:

I remember sitting at a missions' conference when a fellow missionary stood before a church and made a bold request—he asked for $1,000,000 to build 10 churches... all inside one building. It caught everyone off guard. There were no details, no clear plan, no strategy for leadership development or sustainability—just a big number and a vague idea. As I listened, I couldn't help but feel the disconnect. It wasn't just the size of the request—it was the lack of clarity and vision behind it. Church planting isn't about flashy figures or ambitious headlines. It's about people. It's about long-term discipleship, cultural sensitivity, and wise stewardship. What that missionary presented wasn't a vision—it was a dream without direction. And in missions, when you're asking others to invest their prayers, resources, and trust, clarity isn't optional—it's essential. A compelling vision must be specific, Spirit-led, and realistic. That moment reminded me that people don't respond to numbers—they respond to purpose. Don't ask for a million dollars. Show them what God wants to do with every soul, every village, and every church. Let the vision speak—and let it be clear.

Pre-launch costs
- Gear
- Promotion
- Events

Monthly operations
- Rent
- Supplies
- Admin

Ministry
- Kids
- Outreach
- Discipleship tools

Margin
- For the unexpected (But be practical)

I once followed a missionary on social media who seemed to post a new financial request every week—not for ministry needs, but for broken personal items. One week it was a cracked phone screen, the next week it was a tire replacement, then a washing machine that stopped working. Over time, the pattern became hard to ignore. What began as updates turned into a constant stream of financial appeals. Eventually, someone publicly called him out—not in anger, but in honest concern. They asked, "Is this how you want people to see the mission? As one long list of broken stuff?" That moment stuck with me. It reminded me that while transparency is important, so is discretion. Social media is a powerful tool, but it should be used wisely. Personal needs are often best shared privately—with close supporters or sending churches—while social media can be reserved for celebrating God's faithfulness, sharing testimonies, and occasionally inviting help for truly unexpected or urgent situations. Steward your voice well. The way we present the mission matters—and sometimes the greatest support comes from quiet conversations, not public posts.

5. Set Up Smart Financial Systems

Before receiving funds:
- Open a church bank account
- Use accounting software
- Set up giving platforms (online, mobile)
- Appoint a treasurer or financial overseer
- Plan annual budgets and reports

Note:
Even in our remote villages in Africa every church has a bank account in the name of the church and not the pastor.

Financial integrity builds credibility for the mission.

In church planting and missions, how you handle money speaks just as loudly as how you preach the Gospel. People may support your vision, but they stay invested when they trust your character. Financial integrity isn't just about keeping receipts—it's about building trust, honoring those who give, and representing the Kingdom with excellence. Over the years, I've learned that supporters don't just want to know what you're doing—they want to know how you're handling what they've entrusted to you. Are you using resources wisely? Are you transparent with budgets? Are you separating personal needs from ministry expenses?

I've seen missionaries lose credibility—not because they lacked passion or calling—but because they blurred the lines between personal spending and ministry funds, or failed to provide clear communication about how money was being used. On the other hand, I've watched ministries flourish when they stewarded every dollar with humility and accountability. Financial integrity becomes a foundation for longevity. It shows you're not just chasing dreams—you're managing God's resources with care and purpose.

If you want people to partner with you long-term, give them more than vision—give them confidence. Keep your books clean. Share updates regularly. Celebrate what God is doing, and let your stewardship reflect your calling. Because when people trust the messenger, they're more likely to invest in the mission.

6. Steward What You Have — Then God Sends More

Note:

I'd like to pause here and share a difficult but important story—one that has stayed with me and taught me valuable lessons about leadership, accountability, and financial stewardship.

I once knew a missionary who allowed a local pastor to embezzle funds from him over time—but rather than confront the issue or remove him from leadership, he chose to overlook it. I didn't know the full backstory at the time. So when that missionary eventually resigned and left the field, I welcomed that same local pastor into our ministry. On the surface, he seemed capable and trustworthy. But in hindsight, I now believe he had grown comfortable taking small amounts of money over time—without correction, without accountability, and without consequences.

Within two years of working with me, that same pastor embezzled $15,000.

What followed was a painful, exhausting one-year investigation. By God's grace—and with the help of local authorities—I was able to recover $6,000 directly from his personal account. The irony and heartbreak was that the previous missionary had set up all the ministry finances in the pastor's name, which made access and control far too easy. And though I was left to clean up the mess, the damage extended far beyond lost funds.

The community where this pastor lives—and serves—lost trust in the church. People walked away, disillusioned and disappointed. Local leaders associated with the ministry faced public shame. And to make matters worse, the very missionary who had once overlooked the problem blamed me for giving the pastor access to funding, and our friendship was never the same. In his eyes, I was responsible for what had gone wrong—when in reality, the cracks had been forming long before I stepped in.

This experience taught me a hard but necessary truth: what you tolerate in leadership today can destroy your ministry tomorrow. Love does not mean looking the other way, and grace does not cancel accountability. We are stewards—not just of money, but of trust, people, and the Gospel itself. I've learned that removing someone from ministry for unrepentant sin is not a failure—it's an act of protection. For the church, for the community, and for the integrity of the mission.

Let this story be a warning. Financial integrity isn't optional. And leadership without accountability will always lead to loss—sometimes more than you can ever recover.

"One who is faithful in a very little is also faithful in much."
— Luke 16:10, ESV

Start where you are. Maybe you don't have much money. But what do you have?

• A house to gather in?
• A car to drive people?
• A speaker or chairs?
• Passion and grit?

Use it. God multiplies what's surrendered.

Story:

One pastor didn't have the money to fuel his motorcycle, so he did the only thing he could—he walked. Step by step, he went door to door through his village, stopping at each home to offer prayer. Most of the people he encountered weren't connected to any church. Yet something powerful happened. They were deeply moved—not by a flashy program or professional marketing, but by the simple, personal love of a pastor who cared enough to show up. He and his team met dozens of people, prayed with complete strangers, and watched as several of them showed up at their launch day. They didn't need a budget—they just needed boldness, compassion, and the willingness to go.

7. Don't Let Finances Dictate Faith

Yes, you need money. But money isn't your master — Jesus is.

Don't delay obedience waiting for a perfect budget. Don't kill vision to play it safe. Ask, plan, then walk in faith.

Some things only fall into place after you take a step of faith.

In the fall of 2023, I traveled to Lomé, the capital city of Togo,

West Africa. There, I met with five local pastors who were faithfully serving and training at the Bible College. I didn't come to them with a big vision plan, an impressive fundraising report, or financial backing. I came with a burden from God and a command that I couldn't shake.

As we gathered in that simple room, I looked at them and spoke plainly: "I have no money to plant five new churches. No donor has written a check. I don't have the logistics figured out. All I have is a clear call from the Lord to move forward."

There was a silence in the room. I could feel the tension between the risk and the invitation. Then I asked a question that would shape all of our futures: "Who is with me?"

Without hesitation, all five pastors stood up. They didn't ask for details. They didn't demand security. One by one, they responded with conviction: "We are on board. We want to go where God is leading."

Their response reminded me of the words in Isaiah 6:8: "And I heard the voice of the Lord saying, 'Whom shall I send, and who will go for us?' Then I said, 'Here I am! Send me.'" These men were ready. They had the heart of pioneers.

I was deeply encouraged, but there was still a reality we couldn't ignore—we had no funding. No visible path forward. Just a yes. But sometimes, that's all God needs.

Within two weeks of that conversation—before we had time to draft support letters or launch a campaign—God showed up. Unexpectedly, miraculously, He provided one hundred percent of the funding we needed to plant all five churches. Every need was covered. Every resource showed up. Not late. Not in pieces. All of it. Fully.

It reminded me of the promise in 2 Corinthians 9:8: "And God is able to make all grace abound to you, so that having all sufficiency in all things at all times, you may abound in every good work."

God didn't just meet the need—He went before it. He had already stirred hearts. Already prepared the provision. But He waited for us to trust Him first.

This experience became a turning point in my ministry. It reinforced a truth I've seen again and again in church planting: provision follows obedience. Not before. After.

"The steps of a man are established by the Lord, when he delights in his way"

Psalm 37:23

Sometimes we wait for clarity, but God is waiting for commitment. Sometimes we want the blueprint, but God wants our surrender.

We said yes, and God moved. He honored the faith of five pastors and one simple act of obedience.

In the end, it's never about what we can afford—it's about who we believe. Philippians 4:19 promises us: "And my God will supply every need of yours according to his riches in glory in Christ Jesus."

Our job is to take the step. His job is to make the way.

"And my God will supply every need of yours according to his riches in glory in Christ Jesus."

— Philippians 4:19, ESV

8. Sample Fundraising Script

(Also known as the five second elevator conversion)

Subject: Help Us Plant a Life-Giving Church

Body:
Hi,
I'm excited to share — we're planting a new church in [City]! Our mission is simple: love people deeply, preach the gospel clearly, and multiply disciples faithfully.
Would you consider partnering with us:

- By becoming a monthly donor?
- By giving a one-time launch gift?
- By connecting us with others who might be interested?

Every dollar helps reach real people with real hope. I'd love to share more if you're interested.

Thank you for believing in us and Jesus' mission!

In Christ,
Mike Napper

9. Reflection Questions

• Have I defined what we need — and why?
• Am I praying consistently for provision?
• Who might God be prompting to give — but I haven't asked?
• Do we have systems for handling money with integrity?

Summary:
God Pròvides for What He Initiates
Church planting takes resources. But God has more than enough. Your role? Ask, plan, steward — and walk in faith.

Provision follows purpose. When your vision is Kingdom-driven, the resources will come.

CHAPTER 4

SPIRITUAL PREPARATION

Before you gather people, raise money, or find a building, God must prepare you.

You're not starting a project. You're stepping into a spiritual battle, a personal crucible, and a divine assignment. Success in church planting doesn't begin with a strategy — it begins with a surrendered heart.

> *"Unless the Lord builds the house, those who build it labor in vain."*
>
> — Psalm 127:1, ESV

Spiritual preparation isn't a one-time event. It's a daily rhythm, the foundation of all you hope to build.

You don't prepare spiritually for church planting by attending a conference, reading a book, or setting aside a weekend for prayer and fasting—though all of those can be valuable. Real spiritual preparation happens in the quiet, consistent, often unseen moments of daily surrender. It's in the early morning hours when you open your Bible, not to prepare a sermon, but to prepare your heart. It's in the long walks where you talk with God about your fears, your hopes, and your obedience. It's in the continual dying to self when things don't go as planned, when people disappoint you, or when the weight of the mission feels like too much to carry alone.

In my own journey, I've learned that planting churches and training pastors is not just a physical or strategic task—it's spiritual warfare. You're not just building buildings and raising leaders; you're tearing down strongholds, invading darkness, and reclaiming territory for the Kingdom of God. That kind of work cannot be done with yesterday's strength. You need fresh oil, fresh fire, and fresh direction from the Holy Spirit every single day.

If you neglect your spiritual preparation, everything else you build will be on shaky ground. But if you remain rooted—anchored in God's Word, guided by His Spirit, and aligned with His will—then even when the storms come (and they will), the work will endure. Don't treat your devotional life like a box to check—treat it like the fuel that keeps the mission alive. Because the foundation you lay in the secret place will determine the fruit you see in the public space.

More often than not, it's the prior spiritual preparation—the quiet seasons of prayer, fasting, and seeking God—that sets the stage for what looks like a "sudden" church plant. From the outside, it may seem accidental, even spontaneous. People might say, "How did that come together so fast?" or "What perfect timing!" But behind those divine moments is often a long trail of obedience, surrender, and spiritual groundwork.

I've seen it time and again in my own ministry. God positions you in the right place at the right time, opens the right doors, brings the right people, and provides in ways you couldn't have planned. And when it happens, it feels like a divine surprise—but it's really the fruit of being spiritually ready before the opportunity arrives.

The Holy Spirit honors preparation. And when you've been walking closely with God—listening, praying, staying available—He often launches churches in ways you never could have orchestrated yourself. It's not accidental. It's alignment. And it only happens when the planter is spiritually prepared to move when God says, "Now."

On more than one occasion, I've found myself in a village conducting a Vacation Bible School or showing the Jesus Film, simply being faithful to share the Gospel and love people well. And more than once, something remarkable has happened. The village chief—often unannounced—would approach me during or after the event and say something that still humbles me every time: "Thank you for bringing the true message of God to our village." Then, almost without hesitation, he would add, "I want to give you land and help launch this church with you."

These weren't conversations I initiated. I wasn't there to ask for land or negotiate property. I was simply there to sow the seed of the Gospel. But God was already working ahead of us—stirring hearts, opening doors, and softening the ground. These moments have reminded me that when we stay focused on the mission of reaching people, God often surprises us with provision we didn't even ask for. Chiefs offering land, communities welcoming churches—these are not the result of clever strategies, but of spiritual preparation, relational trust, and God's divine timing. It's His harvest—we just get to be part of it.

1. The Spiritual Weight of Church Planting

Church planting exposes every weakness. It tests your marriage, identity, faith, and endurance. It will push you beyond your limits and into total dependence on God.

Ask any planter:
- It's more spiritual than they expected.
- It's more emotionally draining than they were warned.
- It's more dependent on prayer than they planned.

But God uses the pressure to refine you, not crush you.

Church planting—especially in difficult or unreached places—comes with a kind of pressure you can't fully prepare for. There's financial pressure, relational strain, spiritual warfare, and the constant weight of responsibility. At times, it can feel overwhelming, like you're being squeezed from every side. You may wonder if you're cut out for it or if you'll make it through. I've had those moments myself—days when quitting seemed easier than continuing.

But here's what I've learned: that pressure is not meant to destroy you—it's meant to refine you. It exposes what's weak, but it also strengthens what's true. It burns away pride, impatience, and self-reliance, and it drives you deeper into dependence on God. The pressure forms endurance. It purifies motives. It shapes your character so that what you're building on the outside can be sustained by what God is forming on the inside.

Much like gold in the fire or a diamond underweight, the pressure doesn't remove your value—it reveals it. So don't run from the hard moments. Don't misinterpret the struggle as failure. If God called you to plant, then He's also using every challenge to prepare you for the fruit ahead. The pressure may be intense, but in the hands of the Refiner, it's producing something eternal.

Because of this shift—learning to trust God through the pressure, refining our methods, and focusing on training leaders rather than doing it all ourselves—we went from planting a church every few years to planting many churches in a single year. What once felt slow and labor-intensive began to multiply quickly. As we empowered local pastors, trained missionaries, and relied on the Holy Spirit more than our own strength, the pace of multiplication increased dramatically. It wasn't because we found a shortcut—it was because we embraced the process, allowed God to refine us, and aligned our mission with His strategy. What had once been a trickle became a movement. Church planting no longer depended on one person or one plan—it became a team effort fueled by obedience, faith, and God's perfect timing.

> *"Not by might, nor by power, but by my Spirit, says the Lord of hosts."*
>
> — Zechariah 4:6, ESV

2. Build Yourself Before You Build the Church

You can't lead others where you haven't gone.

This truth is at the core of authentic leadership—especially in church planting and missions. You can teach what you know, but you reproduce who you are. If you haven't walked through the fire of obedience, you can't guide others through it. If you haven't learned to trust God with nothing, you can't disciple someone else to live by faith. If you haven't been shaped by the pressure, the hardship, and the unseen sacrifices, you'll only be able to offer surface-level advice when others face those same challenges.

In my own journey, I've learned that people don't just need information—they need examples. The pastors and missionaries I train are watching how I live, not just listening to what I say. They can tell whether the lessons I teach are coming from real experience or just theory. That's why spiritual preparation, personal sacrifice, and deep intimacy with God aren't optional— they're essential. Your journey becomes their pathway. Your scars become their wisdom. Your faith becomes their fuel.

Leadership in the Kingdom isn't about titles—it's about testimony. So before you try to take others somewhere, ask yourself: have I gone there first? Have I allowed God to lead me in the very areas I'm calling others to follow? Because true multiplication doesn't begin with words—it begins with your walk.

Local pastors often tell me that they trust and follow me—not because of what I say, but because of what I do. It's not just the sermons or the training sessions that earn their respect—it's the way I live alongside them. It's preaching Christ one day and climbing onto a tractor the next to help build a road for the village. They see that I'm not above the work—I'm in it with them. That kind of example speaks louder than any message. It builds trust, strengthens unity, and models the kind of servant leadership that reflects Jesus. In their eyes, I'm not just a missionary—I'm a brother in the work, and that's what opens hearts and moves the mission forward.

Build:
- A consistent prayer life
- Deep Scripture engagement
- Ongoing repentance and humility
- Spiritual accountability
- Sabbath rhythms and soul care

"Keep your heart with all vigilance, for from it flow the springs of life."
— Proverbs 4:23, ESV

3. Develop a Personal Prayer Rhythm

Prayer isn't optional — it's your lifeline.

A control tower isn't just a part of aviation logistics—it's a lifeline. Pilots rely on it to guide them through airspace they can't fully see. From inside the cockpit, their vision is limited. But the control tower sees the full picture—every aircraft in the sky, every weather pattern, every potential threat. That's why listening to the tower isn't a courtesy—it's critical to survival.

On January 29, 2025, tragedy struck when a U.S. Army Blackhawk helicopter collided mid-air with an American Airlines passenger plane over Washington, D.C. Everyone on board the helicopter and plane was killed. The crash was not caused by mechanical failure or enemy fire—it was the result of miscommunication and a failure to follow air traffic control instructions. The pilot of the Blackhawk didn't heed the control tower's commands. She moved into restricted airspace, and within moments, two aircraft collided in the sky.

This wasn't just a tragic accident—it was a sobering reminder of what happens when someone refuses to listen to the one who sees what they cannot.

In ministry and church planting, we are like pilots. We may have training, vision, and passion—but we still only see a part of the picture. God is the one in the control tower. He sees the timing, the territory, the obstacles, and the unseen spiritual battles around us. And just like that pilot, if we rush ahead without listening—if we think we know better or act without waiting for His command—we put not only ourselves at risk, but those we're called to lead.

- Set daily prayer times.
- Prayer-walk your city.
- Journal answered prayers.
- Fast regularly for breakthrough.
- Form an intercessory team to cover you.

I once knew a missionary who had a thriving ministry. He was gifted, respected, and bearing real fruit. His church was growing, his team was strong, and his influence was spreading beyond his village. But beneath the surface, he had allowed a private sin to linger—something he believed was small enough to manage, hidden enough not to hurt anyone.He let his guard down, believing no one would ever know. What began as a small compromise quickly spiraled into a devastating fall. The sin led to an affair, and the affair led to a double life—because the young woman became pregnant. Instead of confessing and seeking repentance, he allowed fear and pride to drive him deeper into darkness. Facing the risk of being exposed, he made a horrific decision. He arranged for the pregnancy to be terminated, hoping to erase the evidence of his sin. But that wasn't enough for him.

After the abortion, he lured the young woman down a remote dirt road with the intent to silence her permanently. Armed with a tire iron, he attempted to take her life. But by the grace of God, a local villager happened to witness the attack and intervened, saving the young woman's life. The missionary was arrested shortly after and later sentenced to prison.

That's where sin will take you. It always promises to satisfy, but it only leads to destruction. It never stays hidden. It grows in the shadows until it demands everything—your integrity, your ministry, your freedom, even the lives of others. Satan's strategy is simple: tempt, trap, expose, and destroy.

This story is tragic, but it's not uncommon. That's why every pastor, missionary, and church planter must guard their heart with vigilance. Never believe the lie that "just this once" won't matter. Sin never stays small. Stay accountable. Stay humble. Stay in the light. Because what you compromise in private today may cost you everything tomorrow.

But that's how Satan works.

The enemy doesn't just tempt you to sin—he sets you up to destroy you. First he whispers, "It's not a big deal. You deserve this. No one will ever know." And then, once you've taken the bait, he turns around and shouts, "Look at what they did! Expose them. Humiliate them. Disqualify them." The very sin he tempted you with becomes the weapon he uses to tear down your life, your ministry, and your witness.

That's exactly what happened to this pastor. The sin that started in secret was eventually exposed publicly. And when it came to light, the fallout was devastating. He lost his position, his credibility, and the trust of those he had led for years. His fall didn't just impact him—it wounded his congregation, discouraged young leaders, and gave the enemy a foothold in a place where the Gospel had once been advancing.

It was a heartbreaking reminder that we must guard ourselves at all times. Not just against sin, but against the slow erosion of spiritual discipline and the subtle whisper of doubt. No one is immune—not the church planter, not the missionary, not the veteran pastor.

If Satan can't stop you with opposition, he'll try t

Pro tip:
Don't wait for crisis to deepen prayer. Build the foundation early. You don't rise to the occasion — you fall to the level of your preparation.

4. Invite the Holy Spirit Into Every Step

Don't ask the Spirit to bless your plans. Ask Him to form your plans.

> Roland Allen, The Spontaneous Expansion of the Church (Grand Rapids: Eerdmans, 1962), 7.
> — Allen describes how church multiplication happens naturally when believers are free to follow the Holy Spirit without unnecessary structures.

Pray for:
- Discernment
- Power and boldness
- Divine appointments
- Breakthrough
- Clarity in decisions

Let the Spirit be your strategist.

In church planting, it's easy to lean heavily on strategy—launch plans, demographic research, leadership pipelines, growth models.

And while wisdom, planning, and structure are important, they should never replace the voice of the Holy Spirit. No human strategy can outthink the mind of God. What the Spirit can do in a moment of obedience will far outweigh what your best ideas can do in a decade.

I've seen this firsthand. There were times when I followed a logical path—what made sense on paper, what others had done before—and found myself stuck, frustrated, or out of alignment with what God was doing. But in the moments when I paused to listen, when I allowed the Spirit to direct my steps—even if it seemed counterintuitive—things shifted. The right people came. The right doors opened. The right provision arrived. Not because I planned it, but because I followed His lead.

The Holy Spirit sees what you can't see: the hearts of a village, the timing of a conversation, the soul that's ready for the Gospel. He knows when to speak and when to be silent, when to wait and when to move. If you want to plant a church that lasts—not just in structure, but in spiritual power—let the Spirit be your strategist. Seek His counsel in your planning, your preaching, your relationships, and your decisions.

Don't just ask God to bless your plan. Ask Him to be the plan. When the Spirit leads, the fruit follows. Always.

5. Protect Your Soul from Pride and Performance

Planting tempts you to tie your identity to the church's success. When it grows, pride whispers. When it struggles, shame shouts.

You are not your attendance. You are not your budget. You are God's child.

> *"Well done, good and faithful servant."*
> — Matthew 25:23, ESV

Notice — He says faithful, not successful.

6. Prepare for Spiritual Warfare

Planting a church invites resistance.

Watch for:
- Conflict within the team
- Tension in your marriage or family
- Spiritual heaviness
- Distractions and false accusations

Don't be surprised. Be armed.

If you're planting churches, training leaders, or stepping into any kind of frontline ministry, expect resistance. Spiritual warfare is not a possibility—it's a guarantee. The moment you step into new territory to advance the Kingdom, you become a threat to the enemy. Attacks will come—through discouragement, division, temptation, delays, and unexpected opposition. But the key is not to be surprised by it. The key is to be armed for it.

Too many church planters are caught off guard when hardship hits. They assume something must be wrong. But often, the very presence of pressure is a sign that you're doing exactly what God has called you to do. Satan doesn't waste his time attacking ministries that aren't moving. If you're advancing, you're a target—and that's why preparation matters.

Put on the full armor of God before the battle starts (Ephesians 6:10–18). Ground yourself in prayer. Saturate your mind in the Word. Stay accountable. Keep your motives pure. Cultivate a team that doesn't just work—but watches and wars with you in the Spirit.

Being armed doesn't mean you won't be hit—but it means you won't be taken out. You'll be ready. Steady. Unshaken.

So when the attacks come—and they will—don't be shocked. Be equipped. Be covered. Be faithful. Because the enemy may roar, but he's already been defeated. You're not fighting for victory—you're fighting from it.

> *"Put on the whole armor of God, that you may be able to stand against the schemes of the devil."*
>
> — Ephesians 6:11, ESV

Surround yourself with prayer. Walk humbly, but with authority.

7. Let God Shape Your Heart for the City

Sit in the parks. Walk the streets. Listen to the people.

Ask God:
- "Break my heart for what breaks Yours."
- "Let me love these people like You do."
- "Give me supernatural compassion for this place."

Don't just plant a church. Fall in love with lost people.

For me, it's never just been about one people group, one village, or even one country. I'm not driven by a romantic attachment to a culture—I'm driven by the spiritual reality that people all over the world are dying without Christ. That's what keeps me awake at night. It's the weight I carry every day. I don't feel called to a specific place as much as I feel gripped by the urgency of lostness itself. It doesn't matter if it's in Africa, Asia, Europe, or the United States—if people are living and dying without ever hearing the Gospel, then I want to be part of the solution. I go where the need is, where the doors open, and where God leads—because my heart beats for the lost, not just the familiar. It's not a localized passion—it's a global burden. And until every person hears, I can't rest.

8. Don't Skip the Wilderness

God often leads planters through a wilderness first.

For me, that wilderness looked like trying to learn a foreign language while being dyslexic—an uphill battle that left me discouraged and questioning my ability to serve. On top of that, I was trying to execute a "cookie-cutter" mission strategy I had learned in college, full of formulas and best practices that, honestly, didn't fit who I was. I was imitating someone else's path, not walking in my own calling. And in that season, I felt stuck—

like I was failing at a model that worked for others but didn't reflect how God had wired me.

But the wilderness has a purpose. It strips away pride, assumptions, and pressure to perform. It forces you to listen. And as I kept walking with God through that dry and disorienting place, He began to reveal who I really was—not who I was trained to be, but who He created me to be. He showed me the hidden gifts I'd overlooked, the unique strengths I carried, and how those could be used to spread the Gospel in ways I never imagined.

That's when everything changed. I stopped trying to force someone else's method and started moving in obedience with the gifts God had actually given me. And from that place of authenticity, the fruit began to multiply—churches were planted, pastors were trained, and the Gospel began to reach farther than I ever thought possible.

If you're in the wilderness, don't rush out of it. Let God use it to shape you. Because the identity He forms in the wilderness is what you'll need to carry the weight of the calling ahead.

In the wilderness:
- Motives are tested
- Vision is refined
- Trust is built
- Flesh is crucified
- Dependence deepens

Jesus spent 40 days in the wilderness before public ministry. Don't rush it. Let God prepare you.

9. Key Spiritual Practices

- Silence and solitude — to hear God clearly
- Fasting — to break strongholds
- Scripture memorization — to counter lies
- Sabbath — to resist burnout
- Community — to stay grounded

The health of your inner life shapes the health of your church.

10. Ask Others to Cover You

Invite mentors, pastors, and spiritual fathers/mothers to cover you:

- Pray weekly for you
- Ask hard questions
- Speak prophetically
- Call out blind spots

Isolation kills clarity. Stay covered.

I've always loved being around people—big crowds, energy, conversation, connection. So when I found myself living in a remote village, that natural part of who I am felt stifled at times. The quiet was good for focus, but it also created moments where doubt, discouragement, and spiritual fog would try to settle in. I realized quickly that isolation, while sometimes necessary for short seasons, isn't sustainable for long-term clarity in ministry. Maybe that's why I began inviting short-term mission teams to come serve alongside me. What started as one team a year quickly grew into more than 20 teams annually.

These weren't just visitors—they became co-laborers. Their presence brought encouragement, accountability, and fresh energy. Over time, those teams began to carry out strategic ministry— church planting initiatives, well drilling projects, evangelism outreaches, Vacation Bible Schools, three-day kids' camps, and even hosting full-scale medical clinics. Their partnership didn't just help me stay emotionally and spiritually covered—it helped us multiply the mission on the ground. What was once a lonely village post became a hub of Kingdom activity, because I chose to stay connected, stay covered, and let others be part of the work.

If you're in ministry, especially in remote or cross-cultural settings, remember: you weren't meant to carry the burden alone. Find your people. Invite them in. Let the body of Christ strengthen what God has called you to do.

Summary:
Preparation Precedes Power

You can't shortcut spiritual formation. Church planting is about intercession, surrender, and sanctification before execution.

> *"He is like a tree planted by streams of water that yields its fruit in its season..."*
>
> — Psalm 1:3, ESV

If your roots go deep, your fruit will last. But never forget—the fruit on the tree is not for the tree. It's for those passing by. The fruit you bear in ministry—whether it's wisdom, leadership, compassion, or Gospel impact—isn't meant to glorify you or feed your ego. It's meant to nourish others. Deep roots in Christ produce lasting fruit, but that fruit is always for the benefit of the people God places in your path. Stay rooted, stay humble, and keep bearing fruit that feeds the world around you.

Reflection Questions
- What is God teaching me in this season?
- Do I have consistent prayer and Scripture rhythms?
- Who is praying for me regularly?
- Am I resting in God or striving for results?
- How can I prepare my heart, not just my plan?

CHAPTER 5

IDENTIFYING THE LOCATION

W here you plant matters.
It's not just about dropping a pin on a map and calling it a mission. Every village, every neighborhood, every city carries its own spiritual climate, history, cultural rhythms, and hidden challenges. Some places are ready and ripe for the Gospel—others may be resistant, even hostile. But regardless of the setting, discernment is key. You don't choose your planting ground based on convenience or comfort—you choose based on calling, strategy, and Spirit-led confirmation.

In my experience, some of the most fruitful church plants happened in places that seemed insignificant on the surface. I've stood in dusty villages that didn't even show up on GPS, but because God led us there, the harvest came. Other times, I learned the hard way that planting in the wrong place—without understanding the language, leadership dynamics, or spiritual strongholds—can lead to delay, frustration, or even failure.

Where you plant affects who you reach, how you build, and the future fruit of the work. Ask the right questions: Is this where God is leading? Has the ground been prayed over? Is there a local person of peace? Can this become a multiplying center, not just a static location? The soil matters. The people matter. The timing matters.

Note:

Don't rush the decision. Plant where God points—and you'll see fruit that remains.

Not every good idea is a God idea. And not every open door means it's time to walk through. One of the most overlooked — yet crucial — parts of planting a church is choosing the right location.

A healthy church in the wrong place can struggle. But the right church in the right place, at the right time, can bring revival, healing, and transformation.

We had been working in several villages, searching for the right place to plant a new church. We visited different communities, prayed over them, talked to local leaders, and walked the land. But no matter where we looked, I couldn't find peace about any of the surrounding villages. Every location seemed promising on the surface, but something in my spirit didn't settle.

Then we came across a plot of land for sale — right in the middle of all the villages. At first glance, it felt wrong to me. It seemed too far from any one community, too disconnected to be useful. Frankly, I didn't like it. But the more I prayed, the clearer it became: this was the spot God had chosen. It didn't make sense to me, but it made sense to Him. And so, we stepped out in faith and began building.

Shortly after we launched the church and completed the building, I noticed a massive construction project going up directly across the street. I was curious, so I asked around. What I heard left me in awe of God's perfect plan. They were building the largest soccer stadium in all of West Africa — right across the road from our church! What I thought was an isolated location was about to become one of the busiest, fastest-growing areas in Lomé, Togo.

God knew. He always knows. As Scripture reminds us,

"For my thoughts are not your thoughts, neither are your ways my ways, declares the Lord. For as the heavens are higher than the earth, so are my ways higher than your ways and my thoughts than your thoughts."

— Isaiah 55:8–9, ESV

That piece of land I doubted will one day sit at the heart of a vibrant, expanding community. And our church will be right where God intended — in the middle of the harvest field, ready to welcome thousands who will pass by its doors. Only God could have orchestrated it that perfectly.

> *"And they went through the region of Phrygia and Galatia, having been forbidden by the Holy Spirit to speak the word in Asia. And when they had come up to Mysia, they attempted to go into Bithynia, but the Spirit of Jesus did not allow them. So, passing by Mysia, they went down to Troas. And a vision appeared to Paul in the night: a man of Macedonia was standing there, urging him and saying, 'Come over to Macedonia and help us."*
>
> — Acts 16:6–9, ESV

Even Paul didn't go everywhere he could. He went where the Spirit led him.

I see a trend among many church planters today—they're drawn to areas of major development, places with rising populations, growing infrastructure, and what appears to be strategic momentum. On the surface, it seems smart. It feels exciting. But let me gently challenge that thinking with a simple question: Would you plant an apple tree in the middle of an already thriving apple orchard?

Most likely, the answer is no—unless you're absolutely certain that's where God is calling you. Why? Because in a place already full of fruit, your contribution might be appreciated, but it's not essential. The people already have access to fruit. The fields may be crowded, but they're not empty.

Now consider this—what if you planted that apple tree in a dry, barren place where no one has tasted fruit in years, or ever? Where no one is feeding the people spiritually? That's where your tree will not only be noticed—it will be needed. And the fruit it produces will bring life, hope, and the Gospel to a place starving for it.

Church planting isn't about chasing popularity or comfort. It's about listening for God's direction, discerning where the harvest is truly ripe, and being willing to go where others won't. So before you choose your location based on what's growing fast, ask yourself: Where is the Gospel missing? Who is spiritually hungry? Where can my obedience produce fruit that feeds souls—not just fills a seat?

Plant wisely. Plant intentionally. And always—plant where God sends you, not just where the lights are bright.

1. Prayer Must Lead the Process

The best tool in site selection isn't a map — it's prayer.

While data, demographics, and strategy all have their place, they should never come before seeking the direction of the Holy Spirit. Before I plant a church—or before our national African team or visiting American teams move into a new village—we always begin by praying. We walk through the land. We sit with the people. We ask God for discernment, for divine appointments, and for spiritual clarity.

There's something sacred about prayer walking through a village with no other agenda but to listen. Sometimes, we feel a heaviness in a place—spiritual resistance or the weight of past religious bondage. Other times, we sense an openness, a stirring in the hearts of the people, or a confirmation in conversation that tells us: this is the place. And that's something no map, mission guide, or satellite image can reveal.

Over the years, I've learned that it's not just where we plant, but how we arrive. If we come in with prayer, humility, and discernment, God often opens doors we didn't even know existed. He connects us to key people in the village—a chief, a teacher, a family of peace—who become the bridge for Gospel work. We're not just choosing a location; we're being led to the one He has already prepared.

So yes, use the maps. Do the research. But never let those things replace the voice of God. Prayer is what aligns our plan with His purpose. And when God selects the site, the soil is always ready for planting.

Before you research neighborhoods, ask:
- "Holy Spirit, where are You already moving?"
- "Where is the harvest ready but the laborers few?"
- "What part of the city grips my heart?"
- "Where would we be most useful, not just successful?"

Fast. Walk the land. Drive the city. Let burden precede blueprint.

2. Start with Mission, Not Map

Don't begin with geography. Begin with calling.

Just because a place looks good on the map doesn't mean it's where God is sending you. I've learned that what appears perfect in the natural may come with hidden spiritual battles—but if God has called you there, no resistance can stand against His purpose.

We once thought we had found the perfect site for a new church plant. The land was central, accessible, and seemed like a strategic location. On paper, it checked all the boxes. But shortly after we secured the land, two local witch doctors came to confront us. They were angry—furious that a church was being established in "their" territory. They mocked our efforts and even threatened to kill the two local pastors we had placed there. It became clear: this wasn't just about land. This was a spiritual battleground.

But we didn't retreat. We pressed forward—not with hostility, but with prayer, humility, and love. We built the church anyway, and alongside it, we started a feeding center to serve the children in the community. What happened next could only be described as divine intervention. The very children of those same two witch doctors began showing up to eat at the feeding center. They came hungry for food—but over time, they received something far greater.

Through the kindness of the volunteers and the power of the Gospel, both children gave their lives to Christ.

And that was just the beginning. As their father watched the transformation in their lives—the peace, the joy, the light—he couldn't deny the change. God began to work in his heart. Conviction set in. And eventually, he himself surrendered his life to Jesus. The man who once threatened our pastors was now our brother in Christ.

And yes—our pastors are alive and well. One still ministering in that very village and has already planted a second location while the second pastor has surrounded to missions and is serving in Ghana Africa. What began as a hostile confrontation turned into a powerful testimony of redemption.

This is why we don't plant based on comfort or convenience. We plant based on calling. Because when God calls you to a place, He's already preparing the soil—even in the hearts that seem hardest. So don't let fear, threats, or opposition turn you around. If He called you there, He'll be faithful to finish what He started.

Ask:
- Who are we called to reach?
- What kind of people burn on our heart?
- What community fits our DNA?

Are you called to:
- The poor? (I personally hope so)
- The unchurched? (All of us)
- The de-churched? (Most difficult)
- The culturally diverse? (Today all of us)
- A specific generation or language group? (Again, all of us)

Once you know the who, the where becomes clearer.

Church planting doesn't begin with a map—it begins with a burden. Before you worry about choosing the perfect location, ask God to show you who He's calling you to reach. The mission isn't about buildings or coordinates—it's about people. And once you become burdened for a specific kind of people—whether it's children in remote villages, unreached tribes, urban youth, or displaced refugees—then the location begins to take shape around the assignment.

This is something I've experienced time and time again. There were seasons when I tried to pick the "right" place using strategy alone—considering population density, visibility, access to roads. But none of those factors mattered until I had clarity on the who. Who is God asking me to serve? Who is spiritually starving? Who is ready to hear the Gospel? Once that became clear, where to go was no longer a mystery—it was obvious.

For example, when I began to feel God stirring my heart for children in neglected communities, we didn't just find a church site—we found a village filled with kids who had no one to teach them, feed them, or tell them about Jesus. That "who" led us to the "where," and that's where the fruit began to grow.

If you're unsure where to plant, start with this question: Who has God placed on your heart? When the burden becomes personal, the mission becomes clear. And when the mission is clear, God will guide your feet exactly where they need to go. Let the "who" lead the "where," and you'll never go wrong.

3. Research and Discern

When I first answered the call to missions, I was filled with passion, but I had more questions than answers. The calling was clear—go—but the details? Not so much. And almost immediately, the first thing everyone wanted to know was, "Where are you going?" They expected a city, a region, a dot on the map. But I didn't have one. I only had a deep sense that God was sending me to Africa.

At the time, I didn't fully comprehend that Africa was a continent. Honestly, I thought it was a country. So when people asked, "Where in Africa?" I would reply with all the confidence I could muster: "To the African people." It was my honest answer— and it confused a lot of folks. They wanted coordinates; I had a burden. They were looking for a location; I was feeling the weight of a global call.

But what I didn't realize then was that God was already doing something deeper in my heart. He wasn't sending me to a single village or even a single nation—He was giving me a vision for an entire continent. He was expanding my perspective to see that the Gospel was meant for every tribe, every tongue, every region—and He would show me the specific places in His timing.

Years later, I look back and smile at how naive I was. But I also thank God for it. Because sometimes it's the simplicity of our "yes" that opens the door for the Spirit to lead us further than we ever imagined. I may not have had a map in my hand, but I had a call in my heart. And that call became a journey—not just to a place, but to a people, a purpose, and a continent I now know God had prepared for me all along.

Prayer first — but then do your homework:
- Population density
- Religious demographics
- Community needs (poverty, crime, addiction, education)
- Economic factors
- Cultural makeup

Tip:
Use census data, school reports, Barna studies, and community development resources. Sometimes due to the density of the jungle, I even use a drone.

Ask:
"Can we build long-term mission here?"

5. Consider Strategic Gaps

Some areas are saturated with churches.

That's not always bad, but ask:
- Are there underserved parts of the city?
- Are new suburbs or developments lacking a gospel presence?
- Is there a hungry community few are reaching?

God often calls planters to the margins.
Not the spotlight. Not the city center. Not the places everyone else is rushing to. More often than not, God sends His messengers to the forgotten edges of society—the overlooked villages, the underserved neighborhoods, the hard-to-reach places where few are willing to go but where the hunger for truth runs deep.

In my own journey, I've rarely found God asking me to plant in places where the resources were plentiful and the roads were smooth. He's led me to the margins—where poverty is real, infrastructure is lacking, and spiritual darkness often runs generations deep. These are the places where people aren't waiting for a fancy launch service; they're desperate for hope, healing, and truth. And it's in these margins that I've seen some of the purest expressions of faith and the most powerful moves of God.

Jesus Himself modeled this. He didn't build His ministry in the temple courts or among the religious elite. He spent His time with the outcasts, the lepers, the Gentiles, the broken, the poor. He walked dusty roads into towns others avoided. And that's where the Kingdom of God broke in.

Church planters must resist the temptation to chase convenience, comfort, or clout. Instead, we must tune our ears to the Spirit's leading—and often, He'll point us toward the margins. Because that's where the Gospel shines the brightest. That's where the need is raw. And that's where the harvest is waiting.

So don't be afraid to go where the map fades, where the crowds are thin, and where the name of Jesus hasn't been spoken in generations. That's not the edge of the mission field—that's often the center of God's will.

5. Look for People of Peace

Sometimes location confirmation comes through relational bridges.

Ask:
- Do we know people there?
- Has someone invited us?
- Has someone offered a home, school, or business as a launchpad?

People of peace often hold keys to the community.

6. Test It — Don't Just Theorize

Before committing, spend time on the ground:
- Host a small group or prayer night

• Volunteer locally
• Attend community events
• Spend a full day living like a local
• Host a VBS or Jesus Film

What's the spiritual temperature? Do you sense God saying, "This is it"?

Before you plant anything—before you secure land, raise funds, or gather a launch team—you need to pause and ask one critical question: What is the spiritual temperature of this place? You can study demographics, look at population growth, or even measure social need—but only the Holy Spirit can help you discern what's truly happening beneath the surface.

What is the openness of the people? Is the ground soft or hard? Is there a hunger for truth, or a resistance to it? Is there a spiritual vacuum waiting to be filled, or a heavy darkness pushing back against the light? These questions matter more than location or logistics—because where God is moving, fruit will follow.

I've walked into some villages where, on paper, it made no sense to plant a church. Small population. Remote location. Little to no visible influence. But the moment I stepped foot in that place, I felt the Spirit of God whisper, "This is it." And those moments led to powerful breakthroughs. Lives changed. Churches built. Entire communities transformed.

On the other hand, I've visited areas that looked ideal—plenty of resources, strong infrastructure, and even some existing ministry activity—but the Spirit said, "Not yet," or "Not you." It takes discernment to know the difference.

So don't rush past this question. Don't assume opportunity equals calling. Take time to listen. Walk the streets. Pray with the people. Sit in silence and ask, "Lord, is this where You want us?" Because when you plant where God has already gone before you, you're not building alone—you're joining a divine movement already in progress. And there's nothing more powerful than that.

I may walk through multiple villages with teams from the U.S. before landing on a spot where I sense God saying, "This is it."

Church planting isn't a race to find the nearest available plot of land—it's a spiritual journey of discernment. I've walked through village after village with American teams by my side, praying, observing, listening, and seeking. Sometimes the people are friendly. The need is obvious. The opportunity is wide open. But still, there's no inward confirmation from the Lord. It's not that the village isn't valuable—every village matters—but we're not called to plant everywhere. We're called to plant where He sends us.

That's why I never rush the process. I've learned to walk slowly, pray deeply, and stay sensitive to the Spirit. We might visit five, ten, even fifteen communities before something shifts—before I feel that still, quiet voice of God say, "This is the one." It's not always dramatic. Sometimes it's a conversation with a local elder that opens the door. Other times it's a broken-down road that somehow still leads us to the right family. Sometimes it's the way a child clings to you, or the way the villagers listen when you pray. It's rarely logical, but it's always spiritual.

When that moment comes—when the team and I lock eyes and know without words that this is the place—it becomes holy ground. Not because of the location, but because of the assignment. And once we sense God's direction, we move with boldness. Because we're not just picking a place—we're stepping into a divine appointment that God has already prepared.

So I walk patiently. I wait prayerfully. Because when God says "this is it," no other village will do.

7. Consider Logistics

Be practical:
- Is there an affordable venue?
- Is parking sufficient?
- Is it accessible by public transit?
- Is it safe for families?
- Is there room for growth?
- Can this village church reach another village

Barriers to access can become spiritual barriers.
When a village is physically hard to reach—due to poor roads, remote location, or lack of infrastructure—it often remains spiritually unreached as well. The harder it is to get there, the less likely someone is to bring the Gospel. But these physical obstacles

often mirror deeper spiritual resistance. If we let access determine our obedience, we may unintentionally leave entire communities in darkness. That's why it's critical to push through the practical barriers—because behind them are souls waiting to hear.

8. Don't Just Choose a Spot — Claim It Spiritually

Once clear, own it in prayer:
- Walk and pray over the land
- Anoint and claim it in Jesus' name
- Intercede over schools, businesses, homes

Don't just rent space. Take spiritual territory.

Church planting isn't about filling a building—it's about claiming ground for the Kingdom of God. When you enter a new area, you're not just leasing land; you're stepping into a spiritual battle. Every prayer, every sermon, every act of love pushes back darkness. So plant with authority, not passivity. You're not occupying a room—you're advancing the reign of Christ.

9. Be Willing to Pivot

Sometimes what looks perfect falls through. A lease fails. A door shuts. That's not failure — that's redirection.

Hold plans loosely. Hold mission tightly.

> *"The heart of man plans his way, but the Lord establishes his steps."*
> — Proverbs 16:9, ESV

10. Plant for the Long Haul

Wherever you land, plan to stay and sow.

Church planting isn't a quick hit—it's a long-term investment. Don't just show up—dig in. Build relationships, learn the culture, earn trust. The soil takes time to soften, and the harvest takes time to grow. Faithfulness over time is what produces lasting fruit.

Influence comes from:
- Deep knowledge of the area
- Consistent presence
- Real engagement in people's lives

Don't think like a renter. Think like a resident missionary.

I train pastors and missionaries not to think like renters—but like resident missionaries.

A renter shows up temporarily, avoids deep commitment, and holds back when things get tough. But a resident missionary settles in, learns the language, loves the people, and invests for the long haul. You're not just passing through—you're planting roots. This mindset changes everything—from how you preach, to how you serve, to how you endure. The Gospel takes hold when the missionary does too.

As a child, I lived in 17 states and attended 42 schools. Yes—you read that right. We were renters, always on the move, never settling long enough to unpack fully or build anything lasting. Sometimes we'd stay in a place for a few months. Other times, only two weeks. There was never a long-term plan. No roots. No permanence. No sense of "home." We were always preparing to leave, which meant we never fully committed to being present.

Looking back, I see how that transient lifestyle shaped my view of commitment and belonging. For a long time, I didn't know what it meant to stay—to plant, to build, to invest in something beyond the moment. But when God called me into missions and church planting, He rewrote that mindset completely.

Now, I train pastors and missionaries to reject the renter mentality. Ministry isn't meant to be temporary or shallow. It requires presence. It requires permanence. It requires us to live like residents, not renters—people who dig in, love deeply, and build something that outlives us.

Because I've lived the difference. I know what it's like to live without roots. And I also know the power of planting them.

Summary:

Don't Just Find a Location — Follow the Call

The right spot isn't always the most affordable or visible. It's where God's call, people's need, and your church's burden intersect.

Discern it. Test it. Claim it. Plant confidently.

Reflection Questions
- Who is God calling us to reach — and where do they live?
- Have we walked and prayed in the area?
- Are we choosing based on convenience or calling?
- What are the strengths and challenges of this community?
- Are we united and excited about this place?

CHAPTER 6

BUILDING RELATIONSHIPS

C hurch planting isn't about programs, platforms, or preaching. At its core, it's about people — and the relationships that connect them.

Neil Cole, Organic Church (San Francisco: Jossey-Bass, 2005), 53.
— Cole reminds us that the church is people on mission, not buildings or programs.

You can have the best worship team, the most dynamic sermons, and a beautiful venue. But if people don't feel known, loved, and valued, they won't stay. And many may never come at all.

Jesus didn't just speak to crowds. He sat at tables. He didn't just gather followers — He formed deep relationships. To multiply the Kingdom, we must first multiply genuine connections.

"By this all people will know that you are my disciples, if you have love for one another."

— John 13:35, ESV

1. Relationships Are the Soil of Discipleship

You don't disciple people by preaching at them. You disciple through proximity, authenticity, and shared life.

Discipleship doesn't happen just from a pulpit—it happens around the dinner table, in the truck during long drives, while hauling water or building a church together, and in those unplanned conversations that happen when you're simply doing life side by side.

That's how I live and lead. With our national pastors and leaders, I don't just teach them from a distance—I walk with them. We pray together, we face challenges together, and we celebrate small victories as a family. They've seen me in moments of faith and moments of fatigue. They've watched how I respond to setbacks, how I care for people, how I raise my family in the mission field. That's discipleship—not just teaching what I know, but sharing who I am.

The same goes for our U.S. teams. When they come, I don't just assign them a task and send them out. I bring them into our world. We eat together, worship together, and sometimes even cry together. We laugh over BBQ at my house, debrief after long days in the field, and talk honestly about what God is doing—not just in Africa, but in their own hearts. That's when transformation happens—not because of a sermon, but because of shared life.

If you want to make disciples who multiply, don't just preach—live among them. Let them see your scars, your prayers, your joy, and your real walk with Jesus. That's how discipleship takes root—and how the Kingdom grows.

The Acts church grew from radical connection:

"And day by day, attending the temple together and breaking bread in their homes, they received their food with glad and generous hearts..."

— Acts 2:46, ESV

That's where real ministry happens — over meals, in homes, in honest conversations.

Some of our most impactful ministry moments didn't start with a microphone or a stage—they started around a table. I remember one evening in particular: we had just wrapped up a full day of work with a visiting U.S. team, dusty and tired, and I invited everyone over to my house for a simple meal. Nothing fancy—just grilled meat, laughter, and good conversation. As we sat around sharing stories, one of our national pastors began opening up about a spiritual burden he'd been carrying for a nearby village. A young American team member was listening closely and felt a deep stirring to get involved. By the end of the night, a prayer team had formed, a strategy started taking shape, and within a few weeks, we had launched a new feeding center at our village Church

That didn't happen in a boardroom. It didn't come from a five-year plan. It was born in the context of shared life. That's how we build—one meal, one conversation, one relationship at a time. When you invite people in, open your home, and create space for authenticity, you're also creating space for the Spirit of God to move. And often, that's where the mission really begins.

2. Be Present Before You Promote

If you want people to trust you spiritually, they must see you invested relationally.

Before inviting people to church:
- Invite them to lunch.
- Learn their name.
- Ask how they're doing.
- Know them and allow them to know you.

Show up at:
- Neighborhood events
- Schools or shelters
- Local businesses
- City council meetings
- Meet the Chief and Grand Chiefs in the areas

Presence builds credibility. Proximity builds compassion.
You can't lead people you refuse to live among. In missions and church planting, showing up isn't optional—it's foundational. It's

your presence that earns trust. People need to know you're not just dropping in to complete a project or take a photo—they need to see that you're willing to sit with them, walk their roads, eat their food, and face the same challenges they do. When you stay, when you keep coming back, when you're consistent in the mundane and the messy—that's when your voice begins to carry weight. That's when credibility is built.

But proximity—being close, available, and involved—does something even deeper. It softens your heart. It erases assumptions. It makes you feel what others feel. When you live near people long enough, their pain becomes your pain, their joy your joy. It's hard to stay indifferent when you've held their sick child, eaten from their harvest, prayed over their land, or cried at their graveside. Proximity doesn't just give you compassion—it gives you shared humanity.

This is how Jesus modeled ministry. He didn't just send messages from heaven—He moved in among us. He built credibility through presence, and He changed lives through proximity. And if we're serious about reaching people, discipling them, and seeing communities transformed, we must do the same. Show up. Stay close. Be present. Let your nearness reflect the heart of a God who draws near.

3. Make the First Move

Don't wait for people to come to you — pursue them.

Jesus went to Zacchaeus. He called disciples from their boats. He dined with sinners.

You do the same:
- Greet strangers warmly.
- Ask good questions. Listen well.
- Follow up personally — a note, a text.
- Bring those on the fringe into the circle.

Hospitality isn't a department. It's a planter's lifestyle.

4. Start a Culture of Invitation

Churches grow when relationships multiply — not just from the stage, but through daily invitations:

- "Come over for dinner."
- "Want to join our group?"
- "We're serving the community this weekend — join us."
- "Let's grab coffee. I'd love to hear your story."

Create a church where everyone is a connector.

She first came to our church as a quiet, unsure young girl—new to the faith, new to community, and unsure of where she fit. But there was something about worship that stirred her heart. She started sitting closer to the front, singing a little louder each week, until one day she asked if she could join the praise team. We gave her a chance—not because she was polished, but because she was passionate. Week by week, her confidence grew. Her heart for God deepened. She didn't just sing; she worshiped. Fast forward a few years, and that same young woman, now 19 years old, is one of the leaders of our overnight kids' camp—a multi-day outreach that brings in children from villages all around. She helps coordinate, teach, and lead worship for hundreds of kids. The same girl who once sat quietly in the back now helps disciple the next generation. This is the fruit of intentional discipleship and giving young leaders space to grow. When you invest early, you don't just build a ministry—you build a movement.

5. Relationships Move at the Speed of Trust

You can't rush deep connections. Some form fast. Others take time.

Be consistent. Be safe. Steward trust by:
- Keeping confidences
- Following through on commitments
- Owning mistakes
- Refusing to gossip

Trust is the bedrock of a healthy church.

6. Eat Together — Often

Jesus did much of His ministry over meals. Meals slow us down. They create space for connection, laughter, and deep conversation.

Strategy:
Host a monthly meal. Invite new guests. Rotate homes or meet in public. Keep it simple, relaxed, and intentional. In Africa we invite them to church on Saturdays to gather water and pray for the villages.

7. Know Names, Not Just Numbers

One of the most powerful things you can say is:
"I remember your name."

Remembering names and personal stories shows people they matter. It communicates value, dignity, and connection. The truth is, I've always struggled with that. Being dyslexic, names don't stick easily for me—and that can be tough when you're trying to build relationships in a culture where personal connection is everything.

Thankfully, in much of West Africa, there's a beautiful custom that helps me out: people are often referred to by what they do. So instead of having to memorize dozens of names, I get to call people by their roles. To them, I'm simply "Missionary." That's who I am in the community. And the lady who sells pineapples at the corner every morning? She's lovingly known as "Miss Pineapple."

It might seem simple, even humorous, but in that simplicity is a deep truth: in missions, what matters most isn't perfect memory or eloquent speech—it's being present, being consistent, and letting people know they are seen.

Build a culture where:
- First-time guests are remembered
- Regulars are known
- No one becomes invisible

Software helps. Intentionality changes lives.

Tools like apps, planning software, and media platforms can streamline ministry—but they can't replace intentional presence. It's your investment in people, not just your systems, that leads to transformation. Real change happens when you show up, listen deeply, and walk with someone over time.

8. Lead with Vulnerability

People don't connect to perfection. They connect to honesty.

I remember a time when we launched a new outreach program in a village—full of vision, prayer, and planning. We brought in a team, set up the space, and expected dozens of people to show up. But only a handful came, and even fewer stayed. The energy was low. The momentum never came. In every measurable way, it felt like a failure. I could've pretended it was a win or talked around it to save face, especially in front of the visiting team. But instead, I stood in front of them and said, "That didn't go the way we hoped. And that's okay."

I shared what I was learning through it—the need to understand the community better, to slow down and listen more, and to never assume strategy alone will bring fruit. And you know what? That moment of honesty connected more deeply than any well-polished testimony could have. People don't connect to perfection—they connect to honesty. That moment gave the team freedom to be real about their own struggles in ministry. It turned a failed event into a meaningful time of growth and unity.

Ministry doesn't always work the way you plan—but God always works through it when you're honest.

When you share your struggles, doubts, and transformation stories, you give permission for others to do the same.

Don't fake strength. Model authenticity.

In ministry, there's pressure to look like you have it all together—to always be the strong one, the faithful one, the fearless one. But the truth is, church planters and missionaries face real battles—exhaustion, doubt, loneliness, failure, and spiritual warfare. Pretending those things don't exist doesn't make you a better leader—it makes you less relatable. What people need most from you isn't a polished image—they need to see your faithfulness through the struggle.

I've learned that my greatest influence often comes not when I'm standing in front of people as the expert, but when I'm sitting beside them as a fellow servant—honest about the days that hurt, the seasons that stretch me, and the moments I don't have all the answers. And in that vulnerability, something powerful happens: trust deepens, hearts soften, and discipleship becomes real.

When you model authenticity, you give others permission to do the same. You create a culture where people don't have to hide their brokenness, but can bring it into the light where healing happens. Jesus didn't choose perfect leaders—He chose available ones. And He met them in their doubt, their flaws, and their fears.

So don't waste your energy trying to fake strength. Your team, your church, and your community don't need a superhero—they need a shepherd who walks in grace, lives in truth, and points to Jesus as the true source of strength.

9. Create On-Ramps for Community

Design environments that foster connection:
- Small groups
- Volunteer teams
- Men's/women's gatherings
- Interest-based meetups

Not everyone connects the same way. But everyone needs a place to belong.

10. Build Bridges Before Services

Don't rush into a weekly service without building relationships first.

Strong plants often start with:
- House churches
- Small groups
- Vision nights
- Monthly gatherings with food, prayer, and storytelling

When relational momentum is high, launch feels like a celebration of what God is already doing.

Summary:
Relationships Are Revival
We don't plant churches to fill seats. We plant churches to connect people to Jesus and each other.
That happens one meal at a time. One conversation at a time. One "how can I pray for you?" at a time.
People may forget sermons. But they won't forget how your church made them feel seen, known, and loved.

> *"Let love be genuine… Contribute to the needs of the saints and seek to show hospitality."*
> — Romans 12:9, 13, ESV

Reflection Questions

- Who in my community needs a personal invitation?
- Am I truly present in people's lives — or just planning events?
- How can our church foster authentic community from day one?
- What rhythms will help us remember names and care well?

CHAPTER 7

STARTING SMALL

T he launch of your church is more than an event — it's the first public step of a new spiritual family. It sets the tone, shapes the culture, and invites your community into the story God is writing.

A great launch doesn't mean thousands in attendance. A great launch means clarity of vision, unity of team, and faithfulness to the mission.

> *"Do not despise these small beginnings, for the Lord rejoices to see the work begin..."*
>
> — Zechariah 4:10, ESV

1. Launch with Prayer, Not Pressure

Before you focus on numbers, focus on presence.

Ask:

It's tempting, especially in the excitement of launching a new church or outreach, to measure success by how many people show up. But numbers don't tell the whole story. I've learned—especially in Africa—that it's easy to draw a crowd. You can offer food, music, or even a well-promoted event and the people will come. But keeping that crowd, discipling that crowd, building the Church—that's something entirely different. That takes presence. That takes God.

So before we plant, we always ask deeper questions:

Have we covered this launch in prayer?

Are we united as a team in both vision and heart?

Are we walking in dependence on the Spirit—not just in my own ideas or plans?

This is especially important when leading national teams. I've learned I must be careful that those I train are not just following my desire, but God's will. I don't want them building something for my sake or because they want to please me. I want them to move forward only when God has given them peace and conviction. Otherwise, we risk building something impressive in size but shallow in substance.

So don't rush toward results. Focus on foundations. Teach truth, model obedience, and trust God with the growth. When the presence of God is the priority, you're not just planting churches—you're planting roots that can weather any storm.

A prayed-over launch has eternal impact — whether 30 or 300 attend.

I'll never forget the night we launched a Jesus Film outreach in a new village. We had planned, prayed, and prepared for weeks. An American team had flown in to serve. Our African team was fully engaged and ready. The projector was set up, the screen stretched between two trees, and the sun had just dipped below the horizon. But when it came time to begin… only ten people showed up.

I'd be lying if I said I wasn't discouraged. After all the effort, all the expectation, it felt like a letdown. I remember standing off to the side, wrestling with disappointment—especially because I wanted the visiting team to experience something big. But in that quiet moment, I felt the Lord remind me: "You're not called to draw crowds. You're called to sow seeds."

And that night, a seed was planted—one we didn't realize would take root so powerfully. From that small gathering, we made a connection with a local man who opened up his land for future gatherings. A few months later, that site became the foundation for a church plant. Today, that church stands directly across from what is now the largest soccer stadium under construction in West Africa.

What once looked like the lowest-attended ministry I'd ever led has now become one of the most strategic locations we've ever planted. And it all started with a small, prayed-over launch. That's the power of obedience. When God is in it, ten people are enough to change a village—and maybe even a nation.

2. Launch at the Right Time

Don't rush. And don't delay out of fear.

God's timing is just as important as His calling. Move when He says move—not just when the moment feels right or convenient. Rushing ahead can cause chaos. But waiting too long out of fear can lead to missed opportunities. Trust His voice over your feelings. Bold obedience in the right timing brings lasting fruit.

Two examples I would like to share:

1. I once visited a missionary in Europe who, during the drive from the airport, spoke with great enthusiasm about the church he had established. Naturally, I was excited to see it in action that coming Sunday. But when we woke up that morning, I quickly realized the "church" he had been describing was actually a small Bible study with just his immediate family in his living room. After five years on the field, he had yet to plant a church. As I spent the week with him, it became clear—he hadn't failed because of lack of opportunity or resources. He hadn't started because he was paralyzed by the fear of failure.

2. I remember meeting a new missionary who had just arrived on the field—he had only been in his country for about a year. He traveled to Togo to attend our pastors conference, eager to learn and connect. I admired his enthusiasm, and he brought along a handful of local pastors he had recently met in his new home country. At first glance, it seemed like he was off to a promising start.

But only eight months later, I received his newsletter. It celebrated the graduation of 30 students from a Bible college he had started from scratch. My heart didn't respond with celebration—it responded with concern. In less than a year, he had launched and "completed" something that normally takes years of relationship-building, trust, discipleship, and spiritual formation.

It was a reminder: don't rush ministry for the sake of results. You might see quick fruit, but if the roots aren't deep, it won't last. Ministry that is rushed for the sake of newsletters, photos, or praise will eventually collapse under pressure. Buildings can be constructed fast—but building people takes time. If you want lasting impact, slow down, dig deep, and let the Spirit do the shaping—not your timeline.

Ministry isn't about speed. It's about substance.

His story reminded me that fear can disguise itself as preparation. You can talk about ministry, dream about it, and even make plans—but until you take action, nothing grows. Obedience requires courage, not perfection.

Key indicators you're ready:
- Core team is solid and committed
- Systems are in place (giving, kids, follow-up, setup/teardown)
- Relationships have been cultivated in the community
- Venue is secured
- Prayer foundation is strong

When the foundation is ready, launch confidently.

Too often in ministry, people either rush ahead without preparation or hesitate indefinitely out of fear. But when you've prayed, planned, and poured into the soil—when the foundation is strong—it's time to move forward with boldness. Don't second-guess what God has already confirmed.

You may not feel ready. You may not have everything figured out. But if the spiritual groundwork has been laid—through prayer, unity, discipleship, and vision—then the time for action has come. I've seen this play out many times in our church plants across Africa. We don't wait for perfection. We wait for the right alignment—when hearts are surrendered, leadership is trained, and the Spirit gives peace. That's the foundation.

And when that foundation is in place, we don't hesitate. We launch boldly—not because we trust in our own strength, but because we trust the One who built the foundation beneath us. Fear hesitates. Faith moves. So when God says it's time, go confidently. The harvest is waiting.

3. Make It a Celebration, Not a Show

Your launch day isn't about impressing people — it's about welcoming them into the family of God.

Focus on:
- Hospitality: Every guest should feel valued.
- Simplicity: Clear, Christ-centered worship and teaching.
- Connection: Make it easy for people to take a next step (groups, prayer, serving).

Don't overcomplicate it. Make it warm, authentic, and Spirit-filled.

4. Promote Relationally, Not Just Digitally

Use tools like social media, websites, and mailers — but don't rely on them alone.

Even here in Africa, I use social media and websites to help spread the word when launching a new church. These tools allow us to reach more people, share vision, and keep supporters and local contacts informed. But no matter how much technology we use, I've learned something very important: nothing replaces a personal invitation.

That's why, in every village where we plant a church, I still go door-to-door, hand-delivering invitations. There's no mail system in these areas, and many people either don't have access to digital tools or don't rely on them the way others might. So we walk the paths, knock on doors, greet families, and place invitations directly into their hands.

It's not just about logistics—it's about connection. The effort speaks volumes. People respond not only to what's printed on the paper, but to the sincerity behind it. So while I use every modern tool available, I also walk the village roads—because the Gospel moves best at the speed of relationship.

Relational invites are still the most effective:
- Personal conversations
- Friends inviting friends
- Team members bringing neighbors
- Serving in the community in visible ways

Your best marketing is genuine love.

5. Be Clear on Vision

Guests need to know:
- Who you are
- What you believe
- How they can belong

Don't assume people know your heart. Declare it. Display it. Demonstrate it.

6. Prepare for Imperfection

Something will go wrong. A mic will fail. A volunteer will get sick. The coffee will spill. It will rain.

That's okay. Smile. Serve. Stay focused on Jesus.

People aren't looking for perfection — they're looking for presence.

7. Prioritize Follow-Up

The launch is just the first step. What happens next matters more.
- Have a clear plan to contact first-time guests within 24–48 hours.
- Invite them into a group, meal, or coffee.
- Send thank-you notes or texts.

• Keep connection personal, not robotic.

First-time guests who feel remembered are more likely to return.

I once visited a new church plant that had recently launched with high energy and lots of potential. As I entered the small foyer, I was warmly greeted and handed a cup of coffee—something simple, but thoughtful. I was hopeful. I carried that coffee into the small auditorium, ready to worship and observe. But before I could even find my seat, someone approached me—stern-faced—and gave me a firm lecture about how coffee wasn't allowed in the sanctuary.

In that moment, the warmth I felt at the front door evaporated. Instead of grace and hospitality, I was met with correction and control. I finished the service politely, but I never returned. And not long after, the church plant quietly shut down. It never found traction.

What could've been an opportunity for connection became a moment of division—not over doctrine, but over a cup of coffee. It was a reminder that first impressions matter. People don't always remember what you preach—but they will remember how you made them feel. Guests return to places where they feel welcomed, not policed. In church planting, relationship comes before rules—and grace always opens the door.

8. Build for Sustainability, Not Just Launch Day

Don't burn out your team or budget on one big day. Plan for:

This has been a hard lesson for me personally. As a forward-thinking visionary, I'm always looking ahead—already dreaming about the next church plant before the current one even launches. That kind of momentum can be powerful, but if not balanced with wisdom, it can wear down your team and drain your resources quickly.

Early in ministry, I had to learn the difference between a launch day and a launch plan. A big, exciting first Sunday is great—but it's only the beginning. If you exhaust your team, overspend your budget, or put all your energy into one day without a plan to sustain it, the church won't thrive. It may draw a crowd, but it won't build a community.

Now, when we plant, we plan with longevity in mind. We pace our people. We prioritize discipleship. We ask not just, "How do we start strong?" but also, "How do we stay strong?" Because planting a church isn't a sprint—it's a lifelong investment. And your ability to launch well isn't proven by a packed room on Day One, but by a faithful, growing body still gathering years later.

- The next Sunday
- The next month
- The next year

A healthy launch is the first chapter, not the climax.

9. Measure What Matters

Don't just count attendees. Count:
- Connections made
- Next steps taken
- Salvations or baptisms
- New volunteers engaged

Attendance is a tool — not the goal.

Counting people helps you measure reach, but it should never define success. The goal isn't just to fill seats; it's to form disciples. A packed room can still be spiritually empty if lives aren't being transformed. Attendance can guide your planning, but it shouldn't guide your purpose. Use it as a tool to steward what God is doing—not as a scoreboard for your worth. Keep your eyes on faithfulness, not just foot traffic.

10. Celebrate and Evaluate

After launch day:
- Thank God. Celebrate the wins.
- Debrief with your team: What went well? What needs adjustment?

- Stay humble. Stay hungry. Stay prayerful.

"Unless the Lord builds the house, those who build it labor in vain."

— Psalm 127:1, ESV

Summary:
The Real Work Begins Now
A strong launch opens doors. But the real work is in the weeks, months, and years that follow — making disciples, raising up leaders, and multiplying the mission.

Launch well. Then plant deep. Then move to the next one.

Reflection Questions
- Have we prayed more than we've planned?
- Are we launching to impress — or to invite people into God's family?
- What systems do we have for follow-up?
- How will we stay faithful in the weeks after launch?

CHAPTER 8

MAKING DISCIPLES

The Great Commission isn't to plant churches — it's to make disciples. Planting a church is only the beginning. Its ultimate purpose is to form people who know Jesus deeply, follow Him faithfully, and multiply His mission.

> *"Go therefore and make disciples of all nations, baptizing them in the name of the Father and of the Son and of the Holy Spirit, teaching them to observe all that I have commanded you."*
>
> — Matthew 28:19–20, ESV

A church that gathers but doesn't disciple is a crowd, not a Kingdom outpost.

I once sat down with a pastor by the name of Johnny Hunt whose church had grown to over 6,000 people. Naturally, I was curious—How did this happen? When he first arrived, the church had around 300 members. That kind of growth doesn't happen by accident. So I asked him directly, "What's the secret to this kind of multiplication?"

His answer was simple, but powerful: "I disciple those who are willing to disciple others." He wasn't focused on building a big crowd—he was focused on building multipliers. He poured into people who showed a hunger to grow and a willingness to turn around and pour into others. Over time, that investment created a culture of discipleship that multiplied far beyond what any program or event could produce.

What struck me most was that he didn't chase numbers—he chased faithfulness in people. And the result? Numbers came—not because they were the goal, but because multiplication was the fruit of intentional, generational discipleship. It reminded me that the real power in church planting and ministry growth isn't in how many you can gather, but in how many you can equip to go and do the same.

1. Build a Disciple-Making Culture, Not Just Programs

Programs are tools. Culture shapes hearts.

You can have the best outreach, the slickest Sunday setup, and a well-organized calendar—but if the culture of your church doesn't reflect the heart of Christ, transformation won't take root. Programs can attract people and help with structure, but it's the culture—how people feel, how they're treated, how they grow—that leaves a lasting impact. Culture is what people carry with them when the service ends. Build one of humility, grace, mission, and love—and that's where disciples are truly formed.

David Watson and Paul Watson, Contagious Disciple Making (Nashville: Thomas Nelson, 2014), 59.

— The Watsons emphasize simple, reproducible discipleship that fuels movements.

How do you create a disciple-making culture?
- Prioritize relationships over events.
- Model personal discipleship as a leader.
- Celebrate stories of transformation, not just attendance.
- Equip people to disciple others — not just consume.

Discipleship is a way of life, not just a class.

2. Start Small to Grow Strong

Jesus didn't begin with the multitudes. He began with 12 — and spent extra time with 3.

Your first small groups are the seedbed for the culture you want.

Focus on:
- Authentic relationships
- Scripture engagement
- Prayer together
- Accountability and application
- Mission beyond the group

Start with quality. Multiplication follows.

3. Teach Obedience, Not Just Information

Discipleship isn't about filling notebooks. It's about transformed lives.

One of the most powerful testimonies from our ministry is the story of Kife Eko.

Kife was just 17 years old when he gave his life to Christ after watching the Jesus Film during a village outreach. That night marked the beginning of a radical transformation—but also the start of intense persecution. His father, a devout practitioner of voodoo and witchcraft, was furious about Kife's decision. The pressure at home escalated until Kife was eventually kicked out of his house for choosing Jesus.

But that didn't stop him.

We brought Kife under our wing and began discipling him— walking with him, teaching him, and helping him grow strong in his faith. In time, he enrolled in our Bible college and continued to mature not only in knowledge but in character and calling. Today, that same young man who once sat quietly at the back of a Jesus Film gathering has become a bold leader and church planter.

Kife has now helped me plant 12 churches, and he currently serves as a missionary in Ghana, reaching others with the same

Gospel that changed his life. His story is living proof of what happens when we don't just make converts—we make disciples. And it reminds me daily that one soul reached in a remote village can turn into generations of Kingdom impact when we commit to walking the road of discipleship.

> *"Teaching them to observe all that I have commanded you."*
> — Matthew 28:20, ESV

Ask often:
- How is God calling you to obey?
- How can we support you in that?

Knowledge without obedience produces consumers. Obedience produces disciples.

4. Multiply Disciple-Makers

Your goal isn't to disciple everyone yourself. Your goal is to equip others to disciple others.

- Give people simple tools.
- Empower them to lead.
- Provide coaching and encouragement.
- Celebrate multiplication, not control.

Healthy churches release people into ministry.

> *"What you have heard from me… entrust to faithful men, who will be able to teach others also."*
> — 2 Timothy 2:2, ESV

5. Keep It Simple and Reproducible

If your discipleship process requires tons of resources or a theology degree, it won't multiply.

After I gave my life to Christ, I was eager to grow. I enrolled in a discipleship program that was well-structured and full of solid teaching. We went through Scripture, studied foundational Christian beliefs, and learned about the character and calling of a follower of Jesus. It was excellent when it came to understanding what a Christian should look like—how we should live, think, and speak. It gave me clarity, conviction, and direction.

But as time went on, I started noticing something was missing. While the program was strong in comprehension, it lacked application. There was little emphasis on what a Christian should do. I learned a lot about being, but very little about doing. No one talked about sharing the Gospel, discipling others, or stepping into ministry. There was no push to engage the world, to serve, or to plant churches. I had the knowledge, but not the mission.

That experience shaped how I now disciple others. I believe discipleship should always answer two questions: "Who are you becoming?" and "What are you doing with it?" If we only focus on inward formation and neglect outward obedience, we raise up believers who know the Word but never live the Word. My journey taught me that real discipleship leads people not only to look more like Jesus—but to go where Jesus would go and do what He would do.

Ask:
- Can a new believer use this tool?
- Can this happen anywhere — homes, cafés, workplaces?
- Is it easy to pass along?

Simple spreads. Complicated stalls.

Discipleship was never meant to be complicated—but that doesn't mean it's passive or lazy. Simplicity is powerful because it's repeatable. Jesus discipled by walking with people, eating with them, teaching as He went, and modeling what He expected. It wasn't built around programs or perfection—it was built around presence.

We must not confuse simplicity with a lack of effort. Real discipleship means doing life with people. It means opening your home, answering late-night calls, praying with them through hard seasons, and walking with them in obedience. It's messy, personal, and time-consuming—but it's also the most effective way to raise leaders who will do the same for others.

Keep it simple. Keep it intentional. That's how movements multiply. But don't give a pamphlet to someone and say you discipled them.

6. Center on the Word

Disciples are formed by truth, not trends.

> *"Sanctify them in the truth; your word is truth."*
> — John 17:17, ESV

Whatever your structure — small groups, classes, mentoring — the Bible must shape it.

Teach people to:
- Read Scripture daily
- Apply it personally
- Share it with others

7. Make Prayer Central

Disciples pray. Discipleship without prayer is powerless.

Teach:
- How to pray Scripture
- How to pray for others
- How to listen to the Spirit
- How to intercede for the lost

Model it. Practice it together.

8. Lead People to Baptism Early

Baptism is a powerful, public step of discipleship.

"Repent and be baptized every one of you in the name of Jesus Christ for the forgiveness of your sins…"

— Acts 2:38, ESV

Don't delay baptisms unnecessarily. Make it simple, celebratory, and significant.

9. Disciple in Real Life

Discipleship happens in:
- Conversations after gatherings
- Serving alongside one another
- Sharing meals
- Walking through struggles together

Create margin in your life for people. That's where transformation happens.

In ministry, it's easy to fill every hour with tasks, meetings, and goals. But the greatest Kingdom impact doesn't usually happen in your scheduled events—it happens in the in-between moments. When you make space in your life for people—not just programs—you create opportunities for transformation.

Some of the most powerful conversations I've had didn't take place in a pulpit or during a meeting. They happened on the front porch after dinner. In the front seat of a dusty truck driving to the next village. Around the fire late at night when someone finally felt safe enough to open up. But those moments only happen if we have margin—if we're not so busy doing ministry that we miss being the ministry.

Jesus constantly made time for people. He paused for the woman at the well. He walked slowly enough for His disciples to ask questions. He noticed Zacchaeus in the tree. His ministry was full of margin—and so should ours be.

When you create space in your life for people to interrupt your schedule, you're inviting the Holy Spirit to move in ways you can't plan. That's where discipleship becomes real. That's where hearts are changed. And that's where true ministry lives.

10. Remember: The Spirit is the Discipler

You can't change hearts. You can plant seeds, water them, and walk with people — but only God gives growth.

> *"And I will ask the Father, and he will give you another Helper, to be with you forever."*
>
> — John 14:16, ESV

Stay dependent on the Spirit. Let Him lead the process.

Summary:
Make Disciples Who Make Disciples

Discipleship isn't an optional ministry. It's the mission. A church that multiplies disciples multiplies the Kingdom.

If you want to see movement, start with one. Teach them to follow Jesus — and teach them to teach others.

Reflection Questions
- Are we measuring discipleship or just attendance?
- Who am I personally discipling right now?
- How simple and reproducible is our discipleship model?
- Are we releasing people to disciple others?

CHAPTER 9

DEVELOPING LEADERS

A church that depends on one leader won't multiply. A church that raises up leaders can impact generations. From the very beginning of my ministry, this has been my model. I've never wanted to build a ministry around me—I've wanted to build one that outlives me. I learned early on that if the vision is tied to one voice, it stops when that voice is gone. But if the vision is poured into people—through discipleship, training, and shared responsibility—then it multiplies far beyond what any one person could carry.

That's why every church we plant is built with leadership development at the core. I don't just preach and leave—I raise up local pastors, empower missionaries, and train those who will train others. I've seen firsthand how this approach allows churches to thrive in remote villages, in cities, and even across borders—because the mission isn't limited to one man. It's carried by many.

If you want to plant a church that lasts, don't just build a crowd. Build leaders. Because one leader can start a movement—but many leaders can sustain it for generations.

Jesus' plan wasn't just to make disciples. It was to equip and release them as leaders:

"And he appointed twelve (whom he also named apostles) so that they might be with him and he might send them out to preach."

— Mark 3:14, ESV

Church plants become movements when leadership multiplies.

When I left the first country we served in, in Northwest Africa, I didn't leave behind a finished building or even a fully established church. What I left was far more important: trained pastors prepared to carry out the Great Commission. At that time, we sent a missionary we had raised up to Togo, and soon after, a Bible college was established to equip the next generation of pastors, church planters, and missionaries. That intentional focus on leadership is what turned a single church plant into a multiplying movement.

Without trained and empowered leaders, even the strongest ministry will eventually stall. You can have vision, passion, and momentum—but if there's no one to carry it forward, the work becomes stagnant and slowly fades. Buildings don't sustain the mission—people do. And not just any people, but leaders who are discipled, trusted, and sent.

That's why leadership development is never an afterthought in our church plants—it's the foundation. Because when leaders are multiplied, movements are born. This has not been replicated in other countries we are working in.

1. Leadership Development Starts with Intentionality

You don't stumble into multiplication. You plan for it. Below is an excerpt of an article written in Southern Baptist Church (SBC) Life about a Pastor friend of mine by the name of Dr. Danny Wood.

In 2002 after taking the church through 40 days of church-wide prayer and fasting in 2001, Dr. Wood presented the *2010 Vision* based on Acts 1:8. This vision challenged the church members to live on mission, give to missions and participate in mission projects.

The goal was that by the year 2010, Shades Mountain Baptist would have missionaries serving in all 24 time zones, plant a church in each of International Missions Board (IMB) 11 global regions, do missions work in all 50 states, adopt New York City to invest church planting resources and plant five churches in the U.S. and one in Canada.

Before the *2010 Vision*, an average of about 240 members went on a total of eight mission trips a year. During the implementation of this vision the participation grew to an annual average of 1300 members participating in 35 mission trips. At the conclusion of the 2010 Vision, the church had people serving and/or ministry conducted in 21 of the world's 24 time zones (the three time zones they missed were in the Pacific Ocean!), ministry had been conducted in all 50 states, churches had been planted in all 11 IMB global regions, seven churches had been planted in the U.S., one in Canada and numerous church planting activities in New York City.

With achievement of the goals for 2010, Wood presented *Touch the World 2015.*

"The *2010 Vision* was a shotgun approach," Wood said. "What we discovered was that we wanted to go into more of a partnership with some of the people we had met, more of a rifle approach. We built this emphasis on the pillars of evangelism and compassionate justice and based it on Luke 4:18-19. In addition to our work with church planters, we came alongside of ministries directed toward human trafficking, homelessness, feeding programs, clean water projects, AIDS, bible translation and orphan care."

During those five years, 6000 members went on mission trips to 17 states and 63 countries and impacted ministries in 5 continents. Also during this time Shades gave 24.6% of their total receipts to missions and ministries outside their church.

Summary: 2002-2021

$38 million invested in our facilities and completed our 20-year master plan while at the same time gave $45million to missions...and now debt free

Over those 20 years Shades has taken its missions efforts to a higher level:

1. Ministry in all 50 states
2. Ministry in 80 countries and 21 time zones

3. Average 1300 people going on 35 mission trips per year

4. Supported 15 church plants internationally and 40 church plants in North America. For us "supporting" is praying, sending teams and providing financial resources.

5. 70 units and 205 people living sent in fulltime missions

Ask early:
- Who am I investing in personally?
- Who shows potential for more?
- What's our pathway for leadership development?

Don't wait until you need leaders to start building them.

2. Look for Heart Before Skill

Talent can't replace character. You can teach skills. You can't teach humility or hunger.

Look for people who:
- Love Jesus deeply
- Serve faithfully when no one's watching
- Encourage and build others up
- Are teachable, not entitled
- Avoid Negative Leaders

"Whoever would be great among you must be your servant."
— Matthew 20:26, ESV

3. Lead by Example

If you want to raise leaders:
Model what servant leadership looks like. Leadership begins at the bottom, not the top. Show up early, serve when no one's watching, and put others first. Let your actions speak louder than your position.

Show humility, integrity, and courage. The leaders around you are watching how you respond under pressure, how you treat people when it's inconvenient, and whether your private life matches your public ministry.

Admit mistakes and learn publicly. When you mess up, own it. When something doesn't work, talk about it. This creates a culture of grace, growth, and honesty.

And for me personally, this has always been my standard: I have never asked a pastor or leader to do something I haven't already done myself. Whether it's preaching in the rain, walking miles to visit a new church, digging a foundation, or praying through the night—if I expect others to do it, I do it first. That's how you earn trust. That's how you multiply leaders. Not through commands—but through example.

- Model what servant leadership looks like.
- Show humility, integrity, and courage.
- Admit mistakes and learn publicly.

Leadership is more caught than taught.

This means that people learn how to lead by watching more than by listening. You can give lectures, run trainings, and teach leadership principles—but the most lasting lessons come from your example. The way you respond to pressure, how you treat people when no one's watching, how you handle correction, and how you serve others—those are the things your team will remember and repeat.

People don't just hear your words; they mirror your actions. If you lead with humility, they will value humility. If you lead with boldness and faith, they will take bold steps themselves. But if you preach one thing and live another, what you live will be what they follow.

That's why as a leader—especially in church planting—you must embody the culture you want to reproduce. Your team will catch your spirit, your habits, and your priorities. Leadership development doesn't happen only in classrooms. It happens over coffee, on dusty roads, during late-night prayer, and in the everyday moments where people see who you really are.

So teach leadership, yes—but more importantly, live it. Because what they see in you is what they'll carry into the next generation.

4. Give People Real Responsibility

Don't just ask people to help. Empower them to lead.

There's a difference between giving someone a task and giving them ownership. If you want to build a multiplying ministry, you can't do everything yourself—and you shouldn't. The goal isn't just to recruit helpers; it's to raise leaders. That means trusting others with real responsibility and allowing them to grow through experience.

Whenever we host American teams—whether it's for our Bible college graduation, year-end celebrations, or major events like kid camps at Camp Hope—we rely heavily on our national team. We don't just give them small roles behind the scenes. We place them out front, drawing from their unique skills, gifts, and leadership potential to help plan, lead, and execute these large-scale activities.

This approach not only strengthens their confidence—it strengthens the church. When people are empowered to lead, they grow. And when leadership is shared, the ministry becomes sustainable and scalable.

So don't just give people something to do. Give them something to own. Let them lead, make decisions, and carry the vision with you. That's how movements are built—from the inside out.

- Assign meaningful tasks.
- Let them own ministries or projects.
- Give authority appropriate to responsibility.
- Offer feedback and support — not micromanagement.

Leaders grow by leading.

One of the earliest leadership lessons I learned didn't come from a textbook—it came from experience and disappointment. After graduating from Bible college, I was serving in my local church as the activities director. I teamed up with our lead deacon to create a large-scale discipleship initiative—something we were both passionate about. The goal was simple: help church members discover their spiritual gifts and step into active ministry as they served King Jesus.

We poured our hearts into it, building a full program around the idea of mobilizing the church. We even developed a printed booklet filled with vision, strategy, and tools for evangelism and discipleship. When we brought the finished plan to our pastor for final approval, we were excited and hopeful.

But what happened next left a mark.

He glanced at the booklet, then threw it in the trash. "No one will want to do this," he said flatly. "And if anyone's going to evangelize, it's my job—not theirs."

It was deflating. The momentum we'd built vanished in a moment. That church never grew. The vision died before it could take root. That moment taught me something I carry to this day: if you want leaders to grow, you have to let them lead. You have to trust them, empower them, and give them opportunities to rise. Leadership development doesn't happen in isolation—it happens when people are given real responsibility and space to contribute.

When we stifle leadership, we stunt growth. But when we release people to lead, we give the church a future.

5. Build Layers of Leadership

Movements require more than a few key leaders. They require layers:
- Core team
- Ministry leaders
- Group leaders
- Apprentices and future planters

Each layer supports the next. Each layer multiplies the mission.

In healthy ministry, growth doesn't happen in isolation—it happens in layers. Each person you disciple, every leader you train, every church you plant becomes part of a living structure that supports what comes next. When the foundation is strong, the next level can rise without collapsing under pressure. And when each layer is built intentionally—with prayer, trust, and training—it multiplies far beyond the original vision.

I've seen this play out in our church planting work across

Africa. One pastor we trained discipled another. That pastor then planted a new church. From that new church came a missionary. Now that missionary is training the next generation. Each layer didn't just add—it multiplied. Not by accident, but because every step of the mission was supported by the layer beneath it.

This is how movements are built. Not by focusing on a single moment or one superstar leader, but by equipping people at every level to carry the mission forward. When your strategy is built on layers of leadership, discipleship, and multiplication, you don't just grow—you endure.

6. Create a Simple Leadership Pipeline

You don't need a complex system. You need a clear path.

Example pipeline:
- Volunteer → Team leader → Ministry leader → Trainer of leaders → Church planter

Make it visible. Make it accessible. Make it part of your culture.

7. Coach and Develop Continuously

Don't just appoint leaders — invest in them.

Anyone can hand out a title. But real leaders aren't created through appointment—they're developed through investment. At the core of our ministry is a simple but powerful motto: "If you invest your life into others, it will change the course of human history." I believe that with all my heart, because it's not just a philosophy—it's my story.

I am who I am today because someone took time to invest in me. They saw something in me I couldn't yet see in myself. They didn't just teach me—they walked with me, challenged me, corrected me, encouraged me, and refused to give up on me. That kind of investment left a mark that shaped my life and ministry forever.

Now, I do the same. Whether I'm training a national pastor in

Africa, discipling a young leader, or guiding a missionary team, I don't just hand out responsibility—I pour myself into people. Because leadership isn't about filling roles; it's about forming people. And when you invest deeply in others, your legacy multiplies far beyond your lifetime.

Don't settle for filling positions. Shape people. That's how world-changing leaders are born.

- Meet regularly for coaching.
- Pray with and for them.
- Offer constructive feedback.
- Celebrate growth and faithfulness.

A leader who's supported will lead longer and better.

8. Identify and Train Reproducers

Don't just look for leaders. Look for leaders of leaders.

These are people who:
- Naturally raise others up
- Multiply themselves
- Think beyond their area to the mission as a whole

Equip them to help you develop the next generation.

9. Be Patient, But Be Persistent

Raising leaders takes time. People will make mistakes. Some will quit. Some will surprise you.

Keep sowing. Keep training. Keep believing in people.

"Let us not grow weary of doing good, for in due season we will reap, if we do not give up."
— Galatians 6:9, ESV

10. Release, Don't Just Retain

The goal isn't to keep all your leaders. The goal is to send them.

In church planting and missions, success isn't measured by how many people stay under your leadership—it's measured by how many you've equipped and released to lead beyond you. If your leaders always stay close, your impact remains small. But if they are trained, trusted, and sent, your influence multiplies across cities, nations, and generations.

Every leader we train, we challenge them to follow the ultimate model: be like Jesus in character, lead like Paul in mission, and carry the humility and grace to charm the world without compromising the truth. We don't train leaders to keep them in our system—we train them so they can build systems of their own. So they can start churches, disciple others, reach new territories, and raise up the next generation.

Sending is the heartbeat of the Great Commission. It may feel like loss, but it's actually Kingdom gain. So don't cling to your leaders—launch them. Because when you let go in faith, God multiplies what you've poured in.

- Encourage leaders to start new groups, ministries, or churches.
- Celebrate sending as much as gathering.
- Trust God to provide more as you release.

I've seen too often that some foreign missionaries train leaders to be subject to them, not to God.

Instead of raising up disciples who are empowered, anointed, and released, they create a system where national leaders are kept dependent—spiritually, financially, and organizationally. Out of fear, insecurity, or even jealousy, they hold back the very people they were called to equip. They're afraid the leaders they train might one day preach better, lead better, or reach more people—and so they keep them under their thumb, subject to their authority rather than God's calling.

But that's not biblical leadership—that's control. Jesus didn't train His disciples to be His lifelong assistants. He trained them to carry the mission beyond Him. Paul didn't build an empire—he raised up pastors and church planters and sent them out. If we're truly kingdom-minded, we won't be threatened by the success of those we've discipled—we'll celebrate it.

The goal isn't to produce followers of us. The goal is to produce followers of Jesus who will surpass us for the sake of the Gospel. Anything less isn't multiplication—it's manipulation. Let's raise leaders who are free to follow God, not just us. That's how movements are born.

Sending leaders is how movements are born.

Summary:
Multiplication Requires Leadership Development
Church plants thrive when leadership pipelines flow freely. Make it your mission not to gather followers — but to raise up leaders.

If you raise leaders, your church will outlast you. And the Kingdom will expand beyond what you could imagine.

Reflection Questions
- Who am I intentionally mentoring right now?
- Are we giving people opportunities to lead — not just help?
- Do we have a clear pathway for leadership development?
- Are we celebrating sending, or clinging to people?

CHAPTER 10

MULTIPLYING CHURCHES

P lanting one church is a blessing. Planting many is a movement.

David Garrison, Church Planting Movements (Midlothian, VA: WIGTake Resources, 2004), 21.
— Garrison defines church planting movements as rapid, multiplicative, and indigenous.

Jesus never intended His Church to stop at one gathering, one location, or one generation. The Great Commission calls us to go, to send, to multiply.

> *"And the word of God continued to increase, and the number of the disciples multiplied greatly in Jerusalem, and a great many of the priests became obedient to the faith."*
>
> — Acts 6:7, ESV

Healthy churches don't just add. They multiply.

Too many get comfortable after reaching one milestone—like planting a single church—when that one should only be the beginning of many.

Church planting is not the finish line; it's the starting point of a greater mission. I've seen pastors and planters work hard to establish one church, and once it's up and running, they settle in as if the assignment is complete. But the Great Commission never told us to plant a church—it calls us to make disciples of all nations. That requires multiplication.

One healthy church should give birth to many others. One trained pastor should raise up a dozen more. The first milestone should ignite vision for the next. Comfort kills momentum. We weren't called to settle—we were called to expand.

So if you've planted one church, praise God—but don't stop there. Let that first success be the spark that leads to more communities reached, more disciples made, and more churches established. Because when one church leads to many, the Kingdom begins to flourish across entire regions.

According to the North American Mission Board (NAMB), most church planters in the United States plant a single church and then either remain long-term as the pastor or transition into another ministry role. Globally, the pattern is often the same—unless the pastor is operating within an intentional church multiplication framework. Regions such as Africa, Asia, and Latin America tend to model this approach more consistently. A 2014 study conducted by Exponential and NAMB revealed that only 7 to 10% of U.S. church planters go on to plant a second church.

1. Multiplication Starts with Mindset

From day one, think long-term. Think multiplication. Think Kingdom.

How can we plant again?

Church planting is not a one-time event — it's a mindset. From the first meeting in a living room, under a mango tree, or in a rented hall, we must ask ourselves: How can this become the first of many? We're not just planting a church. We're planting a movement. So we must structure, train, and dream in such a way that planting again is not a surprise, but an expectation. It's not if, but when. The DNA of multiplication must be built in from the beginning — even when our resources are small, our team is few, and our influence is local.

How can we raise leaders who will plant?

A church that grows without raising leaders will eventually collapse under its own weight. Jesus didn't just gather crowds; He invested in a few — deeply, intentionally, and persistently. Our job is not just to build a congregation but to equip the called. Every young believer is a potential planter. Every disciple can become a disciple-maker. Our classrooms must become training grounds. Our pulpits must become launchpads. We must look at the youth group and the children's church and say, "There is tomorrow's apostle, church planter, or missionary." Leadership development isn't optional — it's essential to reproducing churches.

How can we give away what God has given us?

The Kingdom grows when we hold things loosely. God gives resources, people, opportunities — but not for us to hoard. A church that refuses to release will eventually rot. The blessings God has given us — people, finances, buildings, influence — are not for our name, but for His glory. We must be willing to send our best. Give away your strongest leaders. Fund someone else's vision. Share your curriculum, your training material, your worship team, your building — whatever you have. Don't just plant with generosity. Live with generosity. A multiplying church is a giving church.

So, from day one, ask the hard questions. Dream beyond your zip code or your village. Build with future churches in mind. The church you plant today should plant another tomorrow. And the leaders you raise now should be sending others within a few short years.

Let's think bigger. Let's think generationally.

From day one — think: multiply.

Don't wait until you're "big enough." Plan to send before you feel ready.

This is the paradox of Kingdom multiplication: you rarely feel ready. You never have "enough" people, money, maturity, or momentum. But God is not waiting on your perfection — He's looking for obedience and faith.

Too many church plants get stuck because they adopt a mindset of maintenance instead of multiplication. They wait until the building is paid off. They wait until the worship team sounds perfect. They wait until the budget is stable or the attendance hits a certain number. But by then, the urgency is gone. The vision has grown cold. The momentum has faded. And often, the very people who were once passionate about mission are now consumed with managing the machine.

Instead, what if we flipped the script?

What if, while the paint is still drying on the first building, we are already scouting neighborhoods and villages for the next location?

What if, before the chairs are even full, we're praying over a team to send?

What if, while the Sunday service still feels raw and unpolished, we're identifying a young leader and saying, "In two years, we want to launch you"?

That's not reckless — that's faith.

That's how movements start.

The early church didn't wait for comfort or completion. In Acts 13, Paul and Barnabas were sent out while the church in Antioch was still young. The Spirit said, "Set apart for Me Barnabas and Saul…" They didn't say, "Let's wait until next year." They fasted, prayed, laid hands on them, and sent them. Antioch gave away its best — and the world was never the same.

In the same way, we are called to plant again — not when we're finished, but while we're still forming. Not when everything is tidy, but while things are still messy. That's the mark of a multiplying church.

Here's how we're doing it:
- We will build the first location with the second location in mind.
- We'll raise two leaders at a time — one for now, one for next.
- We'll structure our teams to reproduce — not just serve.
- We'll treat every new member as both a disciple and a future disciple-maker.
- We will constantly talk about what's next — because the

vision must outpace the comfort.

It might feel premature. It might feel crazy. But God honors movement. He meets us in the going. When we step out in faith, resources follow. Leaders emerge. Doors open. Miracles happen.

So don't wait until the first building is finished to dream of the next. Don't wait until you feel "strong" to act on your vision. Paint can still be wet, floors still dusty, systems still clunky — and yet, God can still call you to go again.

Multiplication is messy. But so is obedience.

And movements don't wait — they move.

2. Build a Sending Culture

A multiplying church:
  • Celebrates new plants more than new programs. But will use programs to plant more churches.

We celebrate new church plants more than new programs.

Why? Because church planting is the mission.

From the earliest days of the gospel movement, we see a pattern: disciples make disciples, and churches plant churches. New churches mean new lighthouses in dark places. They mean new altars of worship in unreached neighborhoods, new pulpits preaching the Word, new shepherds caring for the lost, and new communities where the broken can belong.

So yes, we celebrate. We throw our biggest parties when a new church is planted. We lay hands on pastors and teams. We cheer for new locations. We rejoice when someone is sent — even when it stretches us. Because the birth of a new church is a miracle, a victory, and a down payment on the Great Commission.

But we're not anti-program — we're pro-mission.

Programs are good. They help us care for people, grow disciples, and meet needs. A thriving church will often have vibrant programs — kids ministries, youth outreach, women's groups, feeding centers, worship nights, recovery programs, schools, and conferences. These are useful and even strategic.

But here's the difference:

We don't exist to build better programs. We use programs to build more churches.

Every ministry is a tool — a means to a greater end.

So, when we launch a new soccer league, we're already asking:

Could this become a church?

When we start a Bible study for moms, we ask:

Could this multiply into a church plant in their neighborhood?

When we hold a youth event in another village, we ask:

Is this the beginning of something permanent — a church that will last?

Programs must serve the mission — not replace it.

Churches that lose the church planting focus often slip into spiritual maintenance mode. They develop layers of activities but lose the urgency of sending. People stay busy, but the gospel stops moving. The church becomes a destination rather than a launching pad.

But in a multiplying church, every program is held loosely and aimed outward. We train our leaders to think beyond the walls. We measure fruit not just by attendance, but by reproduction. We constantly ask, "Where could this lead? Who could we send? What community still needs a witness?"

Programs may fill a calendar — but church planting fills heaven.

Let others focus on building better systems.

We're focused on building new churches.

Let others count programs.

We'll count planters trained, churches sent, villages reached, nations touched.

We're grateful for programs — but we live for the plants.

Because in the end, it's not the programs we'll stand before Jesus and give account for —

It's the souls we reached, the disciples we made,

And the churches we sent to the ends of the earth.

• Sends its best, not its leftovers.
• Prays regularly for new church plants.
• Measures success by sending, not just seating.

Create this DNA from the start.

3. Identify and Equip Planters Early

In your team and congregation, watch for:
- Apostolic vision: they see beyond the local church.
- Evangelistic passion: they love reaching the lost.
- Leadership fruit: they disciple and mobilize others.

Begin training them before they're ready to go. Don't wait for volunteers — call them out.

4. Share the Vision Often

People support what they understand. Keep the vision of multiplication visible:
- Tell stories of church plants often.
- Teach on sending in sermons and groups.
- Involve the church in praying for future plants.
- Celebrate multiplication milestones (groups launched, planters trained, churches sent).

What you celebrate becomes your culture.

5. Develop Reproducible Models

Complexity hinders multiplication. Keep your approach:
- Simple: easy to replicate without huge budgets.
- Scalable: can work in various contexts.
- Spirit-led: adaptable to where God calls.

Whether it's house churches, micro-sites, or traditional plants — build what can multiply.

6. Partner with Networks and Other Churches

You don't have to multiply alone.
Church planting is never meant to be a solo mission. The Great Commission was given to a community — not just individuals.

Jesus sent them out two by two. Paul had Barnabas, then Silas, then Timothy. The early church moved forward through partnerships — leaders locking arms, churches supporting churches, believers sharing the burden and the breakthrough.

And that's exactly what we're doing.

I'm not multiplying alone.

I'm planting churches with the men in our Bible college — young leaders being trained in theology, ministry, and mission. We're not waiting until they graduate to get them moving. We're planting churches as we train. We build the church, and the church builds the Bible college. And through the college, we are raising up more planters, more pastors, more pioneers — men who will go where I cannot go, speak languages I don't speak, and reach people I may never meet.

But it doesn't stop there.

We're reaching beyond our boundaries.

We're helping other missionaries, other pastors, and other countries do the same.

This isn't just theory — it's what we do every single day through Trailhead International Builders. I have the honor of serving as the Director for the Continent of Africa, and our mission is simple but profound:

We come alongside pastors who are already faithfully shepherding a church — sometimes under a mango tree, in an open field, or inside a mud structure — and we help them build a house of worship that will stand, grow, and multiply.

We're not starting from scratch — we're joining what God is already doing. These are men and women who have already planted churches in some of the hardest places on the planet. They've preached without microphones, gathered without walls, discipled without electricity. But their faith is real, and their call is clear. What they lack in resources, they make up for in obedience.

That's where we step in.

We help build buildings — so that churches can build more churches.

These aren't monuments. They're launching pads.

We believe every church we help establish should become a sending church.

We're not just building walls — we're building outposts of multiplication.

And here's what I've learned:

When you're willing to reach outside of your own boundaries to help others build the Kingdom of Heaven, God will reach inside your own work and multiply it.

When you pour into others' visions, God will breathe fresh life into yours.

When you build for others, God will expand what you're building.

That's how the Kingdom works — the more you give, the more God grows.

Trailhead International Builders is a tool in the hand of the Lord. We are not the only answer — but we are part of the answer to the global church planting movement. And we're not just focused on one village, one region, or one denomination. We're focused on the whole harvest.

Because multiplication doesn't stop at your property line.

The true test of a multiplying church is not how many it gathers — but how far it's willing to send, how wide it's willing to serve, and how deeply it's willing to invest in others.

So while we plant churches locally, we also stretch globally.

While we train pastors at home, we build for pastors abroad.

Because this isn't just about our ministry — this is about His Kingdom.

We're raising money to help them build buildings — not just to give them a place to meet, but to give them a base to multiply from. When we see a missionary struggling in another nation, we don't say, "That's not our work." We say, "That's our family." When a pastor has a vision but no resources, we don't turn away — we turn up and ask, "How can we help you multiply?"

This is how the Kingdom moves.

Not by competition, but collaboration.

Not by isolation, but interdependence.

Not by building our brand, but by building His church — together.

If you're planting a church, let me tell you: you're not alone.

There are other workers. There are other warriors. There are partners in the harvest.

We were never meant to do this in silos.

We are a global team, a multiplying family — and every win for one is a win for all.

So, let's plant churches. Let's raise up leaders. Let's send and support and build and bless — not just where we live, but wherever God opens a door.

Because in the Kingdom, multiplication is never meant to be done alone.
- Join a church planting network.
- Collaborate with other local churches.
- Share resources, training, and encouragement.

Unity multiplies faster than isolation.

> "We can never work alone to bring great multiplication. It has to happen through unity & diversity."
> —Loren Cunningham Youth With a Mission (YWAM)

This captures the essence: God doesn't call us to lone heroics, but to unified partnerships across cultures, gifts, and generations. When we walk together in purpose—even amid our differences—the mission expands more rapidly and impactfully than anything one person can accomplish alone.

7. Send Teams, Not Just Individuals

Church planters need more than a vision — they need support.

When planting:
- Send leaders, not just attendees.
- Send prayer and financial support.
- Send short-term teams to help launch.

A team plant is stronger and healthier than a solo plant.

8. Let Go Generously

Releasing people, resources, and leaders is costly. But it's Kingdom economics:

- The more you give, the more God entrusts.
- The more you send, the more God provides.

Don't hoard. Hold loosely. Trust God to replenish what you release.

We've learned this principle firsthand in many of the communities where we serve. In several of our church plants, people don't have steady paychecks or bank accounts. Their income comes straight from the ground—whatever their gardens yield is what they have to live on. And yet, despite having so little by the world's standards, they give with open hands and joyful hearts.

They bring their first fruits—literally. Baskets of tomatoes, bunches of bananas, freshly harvested corn. These aren't leftovers or extras. These are the very first and often the very best of what they have. And they bring it not out of obligation, but as an act of worship.

It humbles me every time. They are not giving out of abundance, but out of trust. Trust that the same God who gave them this harvest will give them another. Trust that they can't outgive the Giver.

It's the kind of faith that reminds me of Proverbs 3:9–10 (ESV): "Honor the Lord with your wealth and with the firstfruits of all your produce; then your barns will be filled with plenty, and your vats will be bursting with wine."

Their example challenges me. It's easy to hold tightly to what we have, especially when resources feel scarce. But the kingdom of God doesn't operate on scarcity—it operates on faith and generosity.

When we hold things loosely, we make room for God to fill our hands again.

"It is more blessed to give than to receive."
— Acts 20:35, ESV

9. Plan for Sustainability

Multiplication must be healthy to endure:
- Equip leaders well before sending.
- Provide coaching post-launch.
- Plan financially to support plants as needed.
- Maintain relational connection — don't abandon what you've sent.

Multiplication isn't a one-time event. It's a lifelong rhythm.

10. Dream Bigger Than Your Church

Your church's name doesn't need to be on every plant. What matters is the Kingdom expanding.

Dream:
- Regional networks of churches.
- Cross-cultural church plants.
- Urban, suburban, and rural multiplication.
- Church planting movements that outlive you.

The goal isn't your fame — it's Jesus' glory.

Summary:
Movements Multiply
If you want to leave a legacy, plant a church. If you want to

change a region, multiply churches. If you want to change the world, raise up planters who will raise up planters.

This is the call. This is the mission. This is the joy.

Reflection Questions
- Is our church committed to multiplication — or comfort?
- Who could we send in the next 1–2 years?
- What models of church planting could we reproduce?
- How can we start praying and preparing today?

CHAPTER 11

SUSTAINING MOMENTUM

S tarting strong is important. But sustaining momentum is what builds lasting impact.

Starting strong is important. It sets the tone, builds excitement, and gives people a sense of direction. But if we're honest, almost anyone can start something with passion. The real challenge is not in launching a church, a ministry, or a movement—it's in sustaining it. Momentum is what turns a spark into a fire, and it takes intentionality, perseverance, and leadership rooted in God's presence to keep that fire burning. Lasting impact isn't built in a weekend event or a powerful launch—it's forged in the quiet, consistent, sometimes grueling work of staying faithful day after day. Movements that endure are led by people who learn to push through the slow seasons, navigate disappointments, and keep the mission central even when emotions fade. The goal is not just to start with energy but to sustain with endurance—because only what's sustained can truly multiply and leave a lasting legacy.

The Apostle Paul is one of the clearest biblical examples of someone who didn't just start strong—he sustained momentum over decades. From the moment of his radical conversion on the road to Damascus, Paul launched into ministry with boldness. But what's even more impressive is how he kept going. Through beatings, shipwrecks, imprisonments, betrayals, and intense spiritual warfare, Paul didn't burn out or back down. He planted churches, raised up leaders, wrote letters, mentored young pastors like Timothy and Titus, and continued preaching the Gospel even while chained in prison. In 2 Timothy 4:7, near the end of his life, Paul could say with confidence, "I have fought the good fight, I have finished the race, I have kept the faith." His life wasn't marked just by a strong start, but by a sustained, faithful run that produced a legacy of multiplication we're still living in today. That's the kind of impact we're called to pursue—not a flash of passion, but a lifetime of endurance.

In the culture I serve in, I've learned that starting something is rarely the challenge—everyone is excited to begin. There's energy, enthusiasm, and a willingness to show up for the launch. But sustaining that momentum, keeping people focused beyond the first meeting, is where the real test begins. It's easy to gather a crowd for something new, but getting people to the second meeting, or to stick with the process until the vision is fulfilled, is a far more difficult task. Consistency doesn't come naturally in every context—it must be cultivated. That's why, as leaders, we have to wake up every day with renewed focus, lead the next meeting with purpose, and keep casting vision for the finish line. We must be both patient and persistent, reminding those we lead that starting is good—but finishing well is where the fruit is found.

Church planting isn't a sprint — it's a marathon.

It's easy to get excited at launch. It's harder to stay focused, healthy, and mission-driven as the weeks turn into years. But it's this long faithfulness that changes communities.

> *"Let us run with endurance the race that is set before us, looking to Jesus, the founder and perfecter of our faith."*
> — Hebrews 12:1–2, ESV

Momentum isn't hype. It's steady obedience fueled by the Spirit.

People often ask me, "How do you do it all?" And honestly—I don't always know how to answer. Because it's not a formula. It's not talent or strategy or hype. It's daily faithfulness. It's waking up, putting your feet on the ground, and doing the next thing God has asked you to do—even when it's hard.

Some days are filled with joy and breakthroughs. Other days, it feels like you're walking through spiritual mud. But I keep going—not because it's easy, but because I know it's from God. I don't operate on adrenaline. I operate on calling. And when your obedience is fueled by the Spirit, that's where real momentum comes from. Not flashy. Not instant. But unstoppable. It's sometimes like the TikTok reel that says "don't ask me how I do it. I just do it and it's hard".

1. Stay Rooted in Prayer

What prayer birthed, only prayer will sustain.

If God places a desire in my heart, I don't overanalyze it—I just do it.

I believe that when you're walking closely with Him, your desires begin to align with His will. Psalm 37:4 says, "Delight yourself in the Lord, and He will give you the desires of your heart." That doesn't mean He grants every whim—it means He plants the right desires in you.

So, when something stirs deeply in my spirit—whether it's planting another church, starting a new program, or moving to a new village—I move forward. Not because I fully understand it, but because I trust the One who placed it there. If it's from God, He'll make a way. My job is to walk in obedience, even when the roadmap isn't clear.

- Keep corporate prayer central — not just individual.
- Call the church to fasting in key seasons.
- Raise up intercessors to cover the church continually.

Prayerlessness leads to powerlessness.

There have been many instances in my life where I prayed over a deep desire, fully believing it was from God. Yet, when I shared it with others—well-meaning people, even spiritual leaders—I was told it wasn't sustainable, not realistic, or too ambitious. But here's what I've learned: when God places a desire in your heart and confirms it in prayer, you don't need human permission to obey.

What others saw as impossible or unwise, I saw as an invitation from God to trust Him more deeply. And because I acted on what He placed in my heart—despite the doubts and dismissals of others—churches were birthed. Not by my strength, but by His faithfulness. Some of the most fruitful ministry we've seen came from moments like that—where obedience to God's whisper outweighed the noise of human reasoning.

You don't need a majority vote when you have a word from God. If He planted the desire, He'll provide the path.

"Prayer isn't just us asking God to fulfill our desires—it's where we align ourselves with His."

E.M. Bounds once wrote, "Our praying needs to be pressed and pursued with an energy that never tires, a persistency which will not be denied, and a courage that never fails." But the strength of prayer isn't found in how hard we try—it's found in how fully we surrender.

When we pray, we're not just bringing our plans before God—we're entering into His. We're learning to recognize what He desires, and to reshape our lives around it. The more we pray, the more our own dreams are purified. We begin to desire what He desires—for people to be saved, for churches to be planted, for the lost to be found.

Prayer is where God's heart becomes our mission.

2. Keep the Mission Front and Center

Vision leaks. People forget. Keep reminding them:

Every Wednesday, after Bible college, we gather for a pastors' meeting—not just to share updates or make plans, but to realign our hearts with the mission. In the busyness of ministry, it's easy to forget why we do what we do. That's why it's so important that we constantly remind ourselves: we're not working for titles, applause, or earthly rewards. We are working for the Kingdom of God. Our reward is in heaven, and the stakes are eternal. People are lost. Souls are dying every day without Christ. Hell is real, and time is short. So we must labor with urgency, with focus, and with the kind of passion that aims to bankrupt hell and populate heaven.

These weekly meetings are not just strategy sessions—they are moments to stir our spirits, to sharpen our vision, and to commit again to the high calling we've been given.

- Why the church exists
- Who they're called to reach
- How their part matters

Preach it. Post it. Celebrate it. A mission-driven church stays vibrant.

I've never visited a dead church that had a real mission vision. Every time I've walked into a lifeless church—one where the passion was gone, the people were disengaged, and the presence of God felt distant—it always traced back to a lack of vision. Not just any vision, but a mission-driven, Kingdom-centered vision that's focused on reaching the lost. When a church forgets why it exists, it starts to die. It may still hold services, take offerings, and follow routines—but without a burden for souls and a drive to fulfill the Great Commission, it's just going through the motions. On the other hand, I've seen small churches with limited resources that were fully alive—because they had vision. They were on fire to make disciples, plant churches, and bring light into dark places. Mission gives life. Vision breathes purpose. When a church catches that, it won't be dead—it'll be dangerous to the gates of hell.

3. Regularly Reevaluate Systems

What worked at 50 people may not work at 150. What served well at launch may need refining.

When we first began planting churches, our strategy relied heavily on visiting teams from the U.S. We would travel from village to village hosting Vacation Bible Schools, showing the Jesus film, and providing rapid food relief. It was fast, impactful, and effective for that season. We were in pioneer mode—training new pastors ourselves, often in the very locations where churches were just being birthed.

But today, things look very different. Now, because we've

planted and established healthy local churches, those churches are doing the work themselves. Our pastors and leaders are walking into unreached villages, starting Bible studies, and from those, new churches are born. The strategy has shifted—not because the mission changed, but because the maturity of the ministry has grown. What once required outside help is now being led by the national church. And that's the goal of multiplication: to see leaders empowered, communities reached, and the Gospel advancing—without depending on the same model we started with.

Every few months, ask:
- Are our systems helping or hindering mission?
- What's confusing, inefficient, or outdated?
- Are we overcomplicating what should be simple?

Healthy systems serve the vision — not the other way around.

4. Care for the Core

Don't lose your leaders to burnout. Check in often:
I don't want to lose leaders to burnout—but I'll be honest, my strategy tends to run at one speed: wide open. When you carry a burden for lost souls and unreached places, it's hard to slow down. The urgency of the mission fuels me. I wake up every day with a fire in my bones to go, plant, train, and send.

But I've learned (sometimes the hard way) that not everyone runs at the same pace—and that's okay. As a leader, I have to recognize the importance of building healthy rhythms for my team. If I don't, I risk exhausting the very people I'm trying to empower. The goal isn't just to run hard—it's to run far. That means investing in rest, building margin, and giving people the space to grow without burning out.

We can stay wide open, but we must also stay wise. Multiplication doesn't come from constant motion alone—it comes from sustainable obedience.

I often joke with our core team that after a full week of big events—hosting an American team, running village outreaches, kids' camps, or church services—we'll finally get a break when the team flies out on Wednesday night. I'll say, "We'll take Wednesday night off… but be ready—Thursday, we're back to work!"

It always gets a laugh, but there's truth in it. Ministry doesn't stop when the visitors leave. The momentum we build during those big weeks needs to be carried forward—and that takes commitment. I've learned that even in the busiest seasons, we can celebrate what God has done, rest briefly, and then keep going, because the mission continues. Rest is part of the rhythm, but so is resilience.

So, ask often;
- How's their soul?
- Are they still clear on their role?
- Do they need rest, resources, or encouragement?

Healthy leaders sustain healthy momentum.

5. Celebrate Small Wins

Momentum builds when you recognize God's hand in the journey.

Celebrate:
- Salvations and baptisms
- Volunteers stepping up
- Groups multiplying
- New ministries launched
- Partnerships formed

Gratitude fuels perseverance.

6. Keep Reaching Out

It's easy to turn inward as a church grows. Fight that drift.
- Continue serving the community.
- Plan evangelistic events and initiatives.

• Challenge people to live on mission at work, school, and home.

Outreach sustains momentum by keeping hearts soft toward the lost.

7. Guard Against Mission Drift

As the church grows, new ideas and opportunities will arise. Stay focused.

Every time we're approached with a new program or initiative, I ask two simple but critical questions:

1. Will this plant a church?
2. Will this make disciples?

If the answer is no to both, we don't move forward with it. It's that clear. We don't launch programs just to stay busy or to copy what others are doing. We launch with purpose. Our mission isn't to be trendy—it's to be obedient. If it doesn't help multiply churches or grow disciples, it's a distraction, not a direction.

In a growing ministry, clarity is a gift. And I've found that when we stay laser-focused on the Great Commission, God brings the right people, the right resources, and the right results.

Ask:
• Does this align with our mission?
• Does this help us make disciples?
• Are we chasing trends or following the Spirit?

Say "no" to good ideas so you can say "yes" to God ideas.

8. Invest in Next-Level Leaders

One of the most important investments you can make in ministry is into the leaders who will carry the mission further than you can go alone. Jesus modeled this by pouring His life into twelve men, and through them, the Gospel spread to the ends of the earth. Movements multiply when leaders multiply. That's why we must constantly be identifying, developing, and empowering next-level leaders—those who aren't just faithful, but also fruitful, teachable, and willing to lead others. As John Maxwell famously said, "A leader is one who knows the way, goes the way, and shows the way." If we want to see sustainable impact, we must not only lead well ourselves but raise up others who will lead with vision, character, and urgency. Don't just lead followers—develop leaders. That's how Kingdom movements are born.

As the church grows:
- Identify emerging leaders.
- Provide training and mentoring.
- Give increasing responsibility.

Sustained momentum depends on multiplying leaders.

This isn't just a leadership principle—it's a core strategy in our ministry. I meet regularly with our national staff, and this is one of the topics we return to again and again. If we want to see more churches planted, we must first raise up more leaders.

You can only go as far as the people you're investing in. Without leadership multiplication, church growth stalls, outreach slows down, and the mission starts to rely on a handful of people rather than the body of Christ. That's not sustainable—and it's not biblical. Jesus modeled this when He trained the twelve. Paul did it with Timothy, Titus, and many others.

In every meeting, I remind our team: if we're not multiplying leaders, we're not multiplying churches. And if we're not multiplying churches, we're not reaching the harvest God has placed in front of us.

9. Renew Vision for Generosity

Early momentum often brings strong giving. But over time, people can grow complacent.

Keep generosity fresh by:
- Teaching on stewardship regularly.
- Sharing impact stories of how giving changes lives.
- Leading by example in sacrificial generosity.

Provision follows vision.

One of the greatest examples I know of a man willing to give everything for the sake of the Kingdom is one of our pastors, Kife Eko. I've had the privilege of watching this man live out what it means to be a next-level leader—not just in words, but in radical sacrifice. Every month, he receives a modest income for his work in the ministry. But instead of keeping it all for himself, I've seen him consistently divide his finances to support other new pastors just starting their journey. He gives so they can go—so they can teach, preach, and plant churches in places he may never reach himself. That kind of selflessness isn't common. It's the mark of a true Kingdom man—someone who understands that the mission matters more than comfort, and multiplication matters more than personal gain. Pastor Kife isn't just leading; he's reproducing. He's investing in others, not for recognition, but because he sees the urgency of the harvest and is willing to pay the price to reach it.

10. Rest Without Losing Momentum

Rest isn't the enemy of momentum. It's the fuel.
- Build rhythms of rest for yourself and your team.
- Teach your church to embrace sabbath.
- Trust God to work even while you rest.

While many people assume I never rest, the truth is—I actually do. My version of rest might look different than most, but it's vital to how I stay focused and spiritually grounded. Almost every morning, around 5 AM, I wake up and cycle anywhere from 20 to 30 miles.

That early morning time has become sacred for me. It's where I clear my mind, pray, reflect, and prepare for the day ahead. It's physical renewal, but also spiritual realignment. In the quiet before the world wakes up, I find strength—not just in exercise, but in the rhythm of intentional stillness with God. That's how I rest... and that's how I keep going.

"In returning and rest you shall be saved; in quietness and in trust shall be your strength."
— Isaiah 30:15, ESV

Summary:
Long Obedience in the Same Direction

Momentum that lasts comes from faithful, Spirit-empowered obedience day after day, year after year. Stay the course. The harvest is coming.

The command hasn't changed—go and make disciples of all nations—and now your church is living that out by multiplying. But don't stop here. Please, don't become the pastor who builds a strong church only to shift into cruise control.

Growth is not the finish line—it's the launching pad.

God didn't call us to maintain. He called us to multiply. You've shepherded a congregation. You've discipled leaders. Now it's time to raise up and release. Plant other churches. Send out pastors. Equip missionaries. Don't just grow your church—extend the Kingdom.

And remember, you don't need to start from scratch. Do what someone once did for you. Just as you were mentored, trained, and empowered to lead, now it's your turn to do the same for someone else. Pass the baton. Train your successor. Empower new leaders to go further than you ever imagined.

Because the mission didn't stop with you—and it must not stop with your church.

Reflection Questions
- Are we still driven by mission, or have we settled into maintenance?
- What's one area we need to simplify to sustain health?
- How am I modeling rest and perseverance for my team?
- Where do we need fresh prayer focus?

CHAPTER 12

FINISHING WELL

It's not how you start that matters most — it's how you finish.

I've heard this quote many times, and while I understand the heart behind it, I'd like to push back just a little. Yes, finishing well is crucial—but how you start also matters, because your beginning shapes who you become along the way. The early days of ministry form your character, your habits, and your dependence on God.

I know the quote is meant to encourage those who stumble out of the gate—and I agree with that grace. Not every launch is perfect. Some of mine were messy, uncertain, and full of doubts. But I also believe that every part of the journey matters—the hard starts, the confusing middles, and the faithful finishes. All of it is part of the story God is writing.

When I look back on the early days of my ministry, I remember plenty of moments where I wanted to quit. Days where nothing worked. Days when I felt alone. But it was in those very moments—when quitting seemed easiest—that God was forming something deeper in me. The bad days shaped me for the good ones to come. And because I didn't walk away, I've now seen fruit that I never imagined back then.

So yes—finish well. But don't underestimate the value of the start, or the refining power of the struggle. The whole journey matters when God is the author.

Church planting is filled with excitement at the beginning. But the true legacy of a planter isn't measured at the launch. It's measured in what remains long after you're gone. Will the churches thrive? Will disciples continue to multiply? Will Jesus' name still be lifted high?

I'm far more concerned with what's inside the church than I am with the building itself—because the legacy of the people will outlast the duration of the building.

Buildings age, crack, and eventually crumble. But the people who are discipled, sent, and empowered inside those walls. They carry the gospel to the next generation—and the next. I've learned that a building might give us structure, but it's the Spirit-formed lives inside that shape eternity.

I don't want to be remembered for what I built—I want to be remembered for who I built. Because long after the roof rusts and the paint fades, the legacy of transformed lives will still be bearing fruit.

> *"I have fought the good fight, I have finished the race, I have kept the faith."*
>
> — 2 Timothy 4:7, ESV

That's the goal: to finish well, with faith intact, and the mission still advancing.

1. Keep Your Eyes on Jesus

Ministry will tempt you to measure success by:
- Attendance
- Giving
- Facilities
- Influence

But those things aren't the finish line. Jesus is. Stay focused on Him:

But those things aren't the finish line. Jesus is. Everything I do—every sermon preached, every pastor trained, every church planted—is not about building my name, but about pointing people to Him. My daily goal is to make someone else better: to help someone become a stronger Christian, a more faithful pastor, a more effective missionary. And the only way I can do that is by keeping my eyes on Jesus and not on myself. That kind of Christ-centered focus changes everything. It removes pride from the equation and fills the work with purpose. I believe this attitude is one of the main reasons our ministry has experienced exponential growth. When people see that the mission is not about ego, but about equipping, they're drawn in—both the lost who are desperate for hope, and the believers who want to volunteer and be part of something bigger than themselves. Jesus is the finish line, the fuel, and the focus—and when we stay centered on Him, the work becomes magnetic and multiplied.

"Looking to Jesus, the founder and perfecter of our faith."
— Hebrews 12:2, ESV

2. Build What Outlasts You

Your job isn't to build your platform. It's to build:

Your job isn't to build your platform. It's to build people—people who will serve Jesus with passion, integrity, and boldness. When we make it our goal to raise up others rather than elevate ourselves, something powerful happens: replication. Every life you pour into becomes another life that can pour into others. That's how movements begin—not through one superstar leader, but through everyday men and women who have been discipled, empowered, and released. If you focus on building people instead of building your brand, your ministry will grow deeper and wider than you ever imagined. The goal isn't popularity—it's legacy. Platforms fade. But people, when built well in Christ, reproduce long after you're gone. That's the Kingdom way. That's real impact.

- Disciples who make disciples
- Leaders who raise leaders
- Churches that plant churches
- Movements that outlive you

Pour into what will remain when you're gone.

I would hate to come to the end of this life—a life God has so graciously blessed me to live—only to realize that all I did was preach sermons, but never truly cultivated discipleship that makes disciples. Jesus clearly commanded us to preach the Gospel to all creation and to make disciples of all nations. Both are essential to the mission. Preaching is powerful—it declares truth, calls people to repentance, and invites them into the Kingdom. But if our preaching doesn't lead to personal investment in people, to walking with them, teaching them, and helping them grow to maturity in Christ, then we've only fulfilled part of our calling. I don't want to be remembered as just a man who preached—I want to be remembered as someone who discipled others to carry the Gospel even further. Sermons can spark transformation, but discipleship sustains it. That's the kind of legacy I want to leave behind.

> *Our eternal investment portfolio should be full of the most strategic kingdom-building projects to which we can disburse God's funds."*
>
> — Randy Alcorn

Randy Alcorn, author of Money, Possessions, & Eternity, reminds us that our greatest legacy isn't measured in buildings or programs—but in people and the Kingdom impact that endures beyond our lifetime.

This quote captures the heart of "Pour into what will remain when you're gone." Your investments in disciples, multiplication, and leadership development will bear fruit long after any program fades.

3. Prepare to Hand It Off

Finishing well means handing off well. Plan for succession before you feel ready.

One of the most important things a leader can do is plan for succession—before they feel ready. I remember times during deputation when we visited churches in hopes of securing support for the work we were preparing to do in Africa. Often, we would walk into a church where the pastor was in his seventies or even eighties, still faithfully preaching and leading. These were men who had built their churches from the ground up and poured their lives into the people they served. But what struck me was how many of them had no clear plan for succession. They loved the church so much that the idea of handing over the reins felt like a threat. But without a plan to empower the next generation, the inevitable happened—many of those churches died with them. It was never intentional, but it was avoidable. Legacy isn't just about what you build in your lifetime—it's about who you prepare to carry it forward after you're gone. If we want to finish well, we must be willing to let go at the right time, and trust God to raise up leaders who will continue the mission.

Ask:
- Who can lead when I'm gone?
- How am I training and empowering them now?
- How can I let go with joy, not fear?

The Kingdom isn't yours to keep. It's yours to steward and release.

I remember one day going to a beautiful fishing pond, excited to catch some fish to take home and eat. And sure enough, I started catching some big, beautiful ones—exactly the kind you'd be proud to cook and serve. But after a few catches, I noticed something strange: no one else was keeping their fish. That's when someone told me—it was a catch-and-release pond. I had completely misunderstood the purpose. I thought the goal was to catch and keep, but the goal was to catch and release. That moment has stuck with me because it perfectly reflects the way the Kingdom of God works. When we sign up to be pastors or missionaries, we don't get the option to hold on to what we build or who we raise up. It's not ours. Our calling is not to collect, control, or keep. Our calling is to steward what God gives us—and then release it, so that it can multiply beyond us. A true Kingdom leader doesn't grip tightly; they open their hands. Because what you release in faith, God will grow in ways you could never imagine.

4. Stay Faithful Through the Valleys

There will be:
- Setbacks
- Disappointments
- Betrayals
- Seasons of dryness

Don't quit. Don't grow cynical. Don't lose heart. Stay faithful in the small things.

Stay faithful in the small things. Ministry—real, Kingdom-minded ministry—is full of moments that test your endurance. Sometimes your efforts seem invisible. Sometimes your plans fall apart. But I've learned to look at life through a different lens: I don't fail—I just find ways that don't work, which helps me discover what does. That mindset has kept me moving forward when everything around me said to give up. It's not blind optimism; it's grounded faith. Faith that God wastes nothing. Faith that obedience in the small things matters, even when the results aren't immediate. What we often call failure, God uses as refining. Every misstep, every closed door, every setback becomes a stepping stone when you stay faithful. So don't despise the process. Stay in it. Keep sowing, keep trusting, and keep showing up. The harvest will come.

> *"And let us not grow weary of doing good, for in due season we will reap, if we do not give up."*
> — Galatians 6:9, ESV

5. Guard Your Soul

Don't finish in burnout, bitterness, or moral failure.

Sadly, I've seen all three—both on the mission field and in churches across America. Burnout from overwork and isolation. Bitterness from unmet expectations and unresolved conflict. And moral failure from unchecked sin or pride. These are real dangers, and they don't just happen overnight. They grow in the shadows of exhaustion, discouragement, and disconnection.

We must stay alert. Satan doesn't just want to ruin our reputations—he wants to destroy our impact. His goal isn't merely to stop you, but to undermine the work God is doing through you. That's why we must guard our hearts, remain accountable, rest when needed, and never let the mission become bigger than our relationship with Jesus.

Finishing well isn't automatic. It's intentional. And it's worth everything.

Stay rooted in:
- Prayer and Scripture
- Accountability and community
- Rest and Sabbath
- Humility and repentance

Finishing well is about your soul, not just your church.

This means that your personal spiritual health matters more than the outward success of your ministry. It's possible to build a growing church, plant multiple campuses, and even become known as a leader—while your soul is slowly unraveling on the inside. Finishing well doesn't mean just handing off a strong organization; it means you walk away with integrity, peace, faith, and joy still intact.

6. Celebrate the Journey

Take time to look back and thank God:

I often pause and reflect on the incredible journey God has brought me through—a journey that began in brokenness. I came from a life of drugs and alcohol, living on the streets, uneducated and headed for prison. I had nothing, and I was going nowhere fast. But God stepped in. He saved me, forgave me, and completely rewrote my story. Today, by His grace, I'm a missionary in West Africa, serving across multiple countries through church planting, Bible colleges, children's schools, feeding centers, sports ministries, and clean water well projects. None of it makes sense apart from the mercy of God. I'm so thankful He made room for me at the table—when I didn't deserve it, when I had nothing to offer. And even on the hardest days, I remain thankful, because even my worst day now is still far better than the life I left behind. God's provision, forgiveness, and calling are more than I could've ever imagined. That's why I keep going—and why I'll never stop saying, "Thank You."

- For the people He saved
- For the leaders He raised
- For the churches He multiplied
- For the ways He changed you

Gratitude fuels faith for the future.

While I am deeply thankful for this journey—thankful for where God brought me from and what He's allowed me to experience—I'm even more thankful that this journey has impacted people for King Jesus. That's what truly matters. It's not just that I was rescued, redeemed, and repurposed. It's that others have come to know Him because of it. The greatest joy isn't in what I've accomplished, but in knowing that lives have been changed, souls have been saved, and the name of Jesus has been lifted high through my story. My gratitude isn't just for my healing—it's for the harvest that came out of it.

7. Leave a Legacy of Sending

The measure of a planter isn't just how many they gathered — but how many they sent.

I would much rather be known as a man who planted an apple orchard than a man who gathered a few baskets of apples. A basket of apples may feed people for a day, but an orchard will feed generations. A few baskets are useful for a moment in time, but an orchard has the power to reproduce, season after season. That's how I view ministry. I don't want to be the kind of leader who just gathers people around myself for short-term results. I want to plant people, equip leaders, and raise up disciples who will go out and bear fruit that remains. Sending is costly—it takes more time, more sacrifice, and often gets less applause. But in the long run, it's the only way to see the Kingdom truly multiply. Because movements don't grow by collection—they grow by cultivation and release.

Make it your joy to:
- Commission new planters
- Release leaders
- Cheer on the next generation

Of the greatest joys in my life is watching a church that I planted go on to plant another church—without my help. There's something powerful, even emotional, about seeing a ministry you once nurtured take on a life of its own. I've watched churches I helped start begin hosting their own kids' camps, their own women's and men's conferences, and launch new ministries completely independent of me. And I'll be honest—it's not always easy. Sometimes it's hard to sit on the sidelines and watch them do what I once led. But that's the goal. That's the fruit of discipleship and healthy leadership. It's not about staying in control—it's about sending others out with confidence. The day your absence no longer limits their obedience is the day you know you've done your job well. Releasing ministry is never about losing influence—it's about multiplying it.

The Kingdom moves forward when we let go.
I've met many missionaries over the years, and I've observed something that breaks my heart: some are afraid to release their leaders. Whether it's fear of losing control, fear of failure, or fear that the ministry will crumble without them, they hold on too tightly. In some cases, churches planted by missionaries aren't guarded with compassion and love—but with control and insecurity.

But here's the truth: the Kingdom doesn't multiply through control—it multiplies through trust and release. If we truly want to see churches grow and movements expand, we must raise up leaders and let them lead. Yes, they might make mistakes. Yes, it might look different than how we would do it. But if we never let go, we're not making disciples—we're making dependents.

Jesus trained His disciples for only three years and then entrusted them with the Church. Paul raised up young leaders like Timothy and Titus, sent them out, and kept moving forward. The mission is bigger than us. When we let go, we create space for others to rise—and that's where true multiplication begins.

8. Let God Define Success

One day you'll stand before Jesus. Attendance numbers won't matter. Budgets won't matter. What will matter is faithfulness.

"Well done, good and faithful servant."
— Matthew 25:23, ESV

That's the finish line. That's the prize.

Summary:
Finish for His Glory
You planted in obedience. You led with love. Now finish with faithfulness. Let your legacy be one of surrendered service and multiplied mission — all for the glory of Jesus.

Reflection Questions
- Am I preparing my church to thrive after I'm gone?
- Who am I raising up to carry the vision forward?
- How is my soul as I near the finish line?
- What would it look like to finish well in this season?

CHAPTER 13

OVERCOMING CHALLENGES

I've had to overcome more challenges than I can count—not because of anything I did wrong, but simply because of the life I was born into. I grew up in a world of social disadvantage and instability. It's no one's fault—it just was. By the time I became an adult, I had lived in 17 different states and attended 42 schools. At one point, we were squatters in Tijuana, Mexico. At other times, we stayed in Salvation Army shelters, lived in foster care, and even scavenged food from dumpsters behind grocery stores.

I was often told—by teachers, friends, and even family—that I would never amount to anything. That I was no better than the trash on the floor. And for a while, I believed it. I quit school in the eighth grade. I was adrift, angry, and full of fear.

But at the age of 18, someone invited me to church. And within months, Jesus met me there. He didn't just forgive me—He gave me purpose. He made a place for me at the table when the world had left me outside. From that moment on, I began walking a new path. Not a perfect one—but a redeemed one.

I still face challenges. I still battle fears. But I've never regretted the road I've walked, because God has used every painful moment to shape me into the person and leader I am today. And I hold fast to this truth: "With God, all things are possible" (Matthew 19:26,

ESV).

Church planting is thrilling — but it isn't easy. Every movement of God will face resistance: from within, from without, and from the enemy.

I once sent a missionary from a restricted-access nation in West Africa to serve in Togo. At first, I was full of excitement watching the passion and enthusiasm this pastor and his family carried. It looked like everything was set up for success. But it didn't take long before the enemy found a foothold. For reasons I still may never fully understand, this pastor and his family fell under the weight of spiritual attack, and everything we had invested— spiritually, financially, and relationally—came to a sudden and painful halt. It was heartbreaking. We had to navigate difficult legal and spiritual realities, all while guarding our hearts from bitterness and burnout. But we gave the situation to God. We didn't quit. We didn't shut everything down. We chose to trust the One who holds the future. And in the months that followed, we saw exponential growth—not only in the ministry, but in the maturity of our leaders. God used what the enemy meant for harm to strengthen our foundation and multiply our reach. That's the nature of Kingdom work: the road is hard, but the harvest is worth it.

Challenges aren't a sign you're doing something wrong. They're part of the process — and so is victory.

"In this world you will have trouble. But take heart; I have overcome the world."
— John 16:33, ESV

This chapter highlights common challenges planters face — and how to respond with wisdom, grace, and endurance.

1. Spiritual Warfare

Whenever the Kingdom advances, opposition rises. Don't be surprised when:
  • Conflicts escalate before a launch
  • Family or health issues suddenly appear

- Anxiety or discouragement creeps in
- Doubts about your calling hit hard

"For we do not wrestle against flesh and blood..."
— Ephesians 6:12, ESV

Fight the real battle:
- Pray and fast regularly
- Declare Scripture over your life and ministry
- Seek accountability and wise counsel
- Worship and rest intentionally
- Surround yourself with intercessors

You're not alone. And you're not powerless.

No matter how isolated you feel or how overwhelming the task ahead may seem, you need to know this: God is with you, and He has equipped you. Church planting, missions work, and discipleship can feel like a lonely road—but the presence of the Holy Spirit is your constant companion, and the power that raised Jesus from the dead lives in you. (Romans 8:11) You may not have all the answers. You may feel underqualified. But you are not without help, and you are never without hope. Heaven fights with you—and that changes everything.

2. Leadership Fatigue

Church planting can drain you emotionally, physically, and spiritually.

Watch for:
- Numbness or cynicism
- Loss of joy or passion
- Avoiding people or responsibilities
- Overwork with little rest

Pace yourself:
- Keep Sabbath and days off sacred
- Set healthy boundaries

- Seek spiritual direction or counseling
- Stay connected to trusted friends
- Learn to say "no" without guilt

Your soul matters more than your stats.

3. Team Conflict or Disunity

I faced team conflict on many different levels—between missionaries, national leaders, volunteers, and even church members. It's one of the most painful parts of ministry, and if left unresolved, it can derail the mission. But through these experiences, I've learned something vital: when we surrender conflict to God in prayer, the Holy Spirit often resolves what our human instincts only make worse.

Team tensions happen, especially under pressure:
- Misaligned expectations
- Poor communication
- Insecurity or competition
- Unresolved sin

"If your brother sins against you, go and tell him his fault, between you and him alone."
— Matthew 18:15, ESV

Face conflict early. Lead with love, honesty, and grace.
Over the years, I've learned that how we handle conflict says just as much about our calling as how we preach or plant churches. I've worked at two different churches where I clearly felt tension building—tension that, if left unchecked, could have led to damaging conflict. But instead of reacting emotionally or fighting for position, I made a decision to honor the office of the pastor and quietly step away.

I didn't leave in bitterness or resentment. I left in peace, trusting that God was redirecting my path. And He did. In both cases, walking away opened new doors and placed me exactly where I needed to be next. I didn't need to defend myself, create division, or make a scene—because I trusted that God was my defender and my provider.

Sometimes leadership means standing firm and speaking truth. But other times, leadership means knowing when to step aside to protect the integrity of the church. In both cases, lead with love, honesty, and grace—and let God write the next chapter.

4. Financial Shortfalls

Tight budgets and financial pressures are common. When it happens:
- Reevaluate your spending
- Communicate transparently
- Teach generosity consistently
- Seek partnerships and support
- Focus on what you can do with what you have

Faithful stewardship invites fresh provision.

5. Volunteer Fatigue

When too few do too much, burnout spreads. Build sustainability:
- Recruit and empower new volunteers
- Rotate roles to provide rest
- Publicly honor your team
- Make serving accessible

Volunteers fuel the mission — protect and refresh them.

6. Slow Growth

Not every plant grows fast. That's okay.

Remember:
- Your value isn't in your numbers
- Faithfulness precedes fruitfulness

• Some soil takes longer to prepare

Ask:
- Are we discipling well?
- Are we visible and serving?
- Are we connecting with guests?

Trust God for the increase.

7. Loss of Key People

When people move on, it hurts — but it's part of the journey.
- Grieve, honor, and release
- Avoid bitterness
- Let it push you to raise new leaders
- Trust God's provision for every gap

The apostles didn't quit after Judas—and neither will you.

Every church will face loss. Leaders move on. Trusted people fall away. Even key pastors may leave for new assignments or unexpected reasons. But no church should be built around just a few individuals. The mission is bigger than any one person.

Use every loss as an opportunity—not just to rebuild, but to grow deeper and wider. Over nearly two decades of ministry, we've experienced this firsthand. We've said goodbye to faithful leaders, sent out strong pastors, and walked through painful transitions. Each time, we felt the weight of the moment. But we also saw the hand of God at work.

For every person we lost, God raised up someone new. He never left us without help. He trained others in the process and taught us to rely not on personalities, but on His power and provision.

The apostles didn't abandon the mission when Judas betrayed Jesus. They regrouped. They prayed. They moved forward. "And they cast lots for them, and the lot fell on Matthias, and he was numbered with the eleven apostles" (Acts 1:26, ESV).

They didn't dwell on the betrayal—they focused on the calling. And so should we.

You may lose people, but you'll never lose God's presence. He is always preparing someone new to step up. Don't let loss stop you—let it stretch you.

The mission continues.

8. Discouragement and Doubt

Every planter will wrestle with:
- "Am I the right person?"
- "Did God really call me?"
- "Is this working?"

Lean into:
- God's Word and your identity in Christ
- Encouragement from trusted voices
- Honest time with God
- Remembering the wins

You don't have to feel strong — you just have to keep going.

9. Vision Drift

In the busyness, mission can get blurry.
- Revisit your mission and values often
- Teach them regularly
- Trim what doesn't align
- Stay focused on disciple-making

Clarity fuels momentum.

10. Comparison

Don't measure your call by someone else's journey. God's calling on your life is uniquely tailored to your gifts, your story, your obedience, and His timing. Comparing your pace, results, or opportunities to someone else's only leads to discouragement or pride. You weren't called to copy them—you were called to follow Him. Stay focused. Stay faithful. God doesn't measure fruit by speed—He measures it by obedience.

I've noticed that many times, a well-known pastor writes a book, and suddenly everyone tries to copy his exact model. And more often than not, they fail—not because they're failures, but because they're trying to reproduce something that God created uniquely for someone else. What worked for one person in one place at one time doesn't always translate the same way somewhere else.

I'm dyslexic, and I also have ADHD—though I personally believe ADHD might just be a hidden spiritual gift! It means I think differently, act differently, and structure my day differently than most people. The way I operate may not be how you operate—and that's okay. That's by design.

So let me say this clearly: This book isn't a step-by-step manual. It's not a plug-and-play system. It's a collection of real stories, biblical truths, and practical principles shaped by experience. My hope is that you'll use it as a reference—not to copy, but to adapt. Let it point you back to Scripture and encourage you to seek God's direction for your unique calling, your context, and your people.

"When they measure themselves by one another... they are without understanding."
— 2 Corinthians 10:12, ESV

Celebrate others. Run your race. Stay faithful where God planted you.

Summary:
Fight Well and Keep Building

Church planting is warfare — but it's holy work. You'll face battles. That's not failure. That's evidence you're pushing back darkness. God is with you. His grace is enough. The promise stands.

"He who began a good work in you will bring it to completion..."
— Philippians 1:6, ESV

Reflection Questions
- Which challenge am I facing most right now?
- Who can I talk to about my struggles?
- What boundary or rhythm needs to be reset?
- How can I keep vision clear during hardship?
- Where have I seen God's faithfulness lately?

CHAPTER 14

ESTABLISHING A LEGACY

Many can plant a church. Fewer can multiply churches. But only a few leave a true legacy — one that outlives them and continues to bear fruit.

This is my deepest burden — and my greatest fear. I don't want to just exist on this playground we call earth. I want to live on purpose, for Jesus. I want my life to count for something greater than myself. I want to know that when my time here is done, I left behind more than just good memories or buildings—I left behind a legacy of disciples who are still making disciples.

I don't fear death. I fear wasting my life. I fear standing before God and realizing I played it safe when He called me to walk by faith. I long to live in such a way that my obedience echoes beyond my lifetime—that churches are still being planted, pastors are still being trained, and souls are still being saved because I said "yes" to Jesus, day after day.

Legacy isn't about being remembered—it's about bearing fruit that remains (John 15:16). And that only happens when we pour our lives into others, trusting that God will multiply what we've surrendered.

Legacy isn't about your name. It's about lives transformed, leaders raised, and the mission carried forward long after you're gone.

"One generation shall commend your works to another, and shall declare your mighty acts."

— Psalm 145:4, ESV

This chapter helps you think beyond today — to build for tomorrow.

1. Lead with the End in Mind

Legacy happens by intention, not accident.

Ask:
- I stepped away today, would this ministry continue?
- Am I building around myself — or around the mission?
- What do I hope people say about this church 30 years from now?

True legacy is what outlives you.

2. Multiply Disciples, Not Just Churches

If you don't multiply disciples, you'll end up with a thousand empty churches—and empty churches eventually become pubs, nightclubs, or forgotten buildings. A church without disciples is just a structure with a name. It may start with excitement, music, and momentum, but without intentional discipleship, it will not last.

Church planting is not about filling seats. It's about filling hearts with the gospel and forming people who will live it, share it, and teach it to others. If the people sitting in the pews don't know how to make disciples, the mission dies with them.

We've seen it happen. Church buildings across the world— especially in post-Christian regions—have been sold off and repurposed because discipleship was replaced with programs, and multiplication was replaced with maintenance.

The call is clear: plant churches that make disciples who multiply disciples. That's how the gospel survives one generation and thrives into the next.

Buildings don't create legacy. Disciples do.

Let This Sink In: Discipleship Isn't Optional

I once did a small personal research project to understand why Islam is currently growing faster than Christianity in many parts of the world. There are many complex factors at play, but one truth struck me harder than anything else:

Muslim men are discipling Muslim men. They are intentional, consistent, and focused on passing their beliefs to the next generation. Meanwhile, in many parts of the Christian world, this kind of deliberate discipleship—especially among men—has largely fallen away.

We've turned discipleship into a class, a pamphlet, or a 4-week program. We've reduced it to a Sunday morning service or an occasional small group meeting. But true discipleship is a way of life, not an event. It's about walking with people, sharing meals, praying together, correcting, encouraging, and equipping them to do the same for others.

One of the greatest threats to the global church is not persecution—it's the absence of biblical discipleship. If we don't multiply disciples, we don't multiply anything that lasts. Programs fade. Events end. But people discipled in the way of Jesus carry the mission forward into their homes, their villages, and the next generation.

Make sure every church:
- Raises up new believers
- Teaches people to follow Jesus daily
- Trains leaders who multiply others

George Patterson, Church Multiplication Guide (Pasadena: William Carey Library, 1993), 45.
— Patterson argues that obedience-based discipleship ensures healthy multiplication rather than knowledge-only gatherings.

"Go therefore and make disciples of all nations…"
— Matthew 28:19, ESV

3. Identify and Train Successors

Legacy leaders raise up others who can carry the torch.

Look for successors who:
- Love Jesus more than the spotlight
- Serve with humility
- Lead with integrity
- Share the vision

Train them. Trust them. Release them.

> *"Choose wise, understanding, and respected men… and I will appoint them as your leaders."*
> — Deuteronomy 1:13, ESV

Train them. Trust them. Release them—at the right time.

One of the most tragic patterns I've witnessed over the years is leaders who refuse to let go. I've seen pastors and missionaries hold so tightly to their role and authority that they never made room for the next generation. They poured their lives into building the church but failed to raise up those who would carry it forward.

And when their time ended—so did the ministry.

In many cases, the church didn't just die when the leader passed away. The decline began long before—when they chose control over multiplication, preservation over preparation. Leadership became a bottleneck rather than a bridge.

It doesn't have to be this way.

A healthy leader trains others to lead, trusts them with responsibility, and releases them when the time is right—not when it's too late. Paul mentored Timothy. Elijah prepared Elisha. Jesus raised up twelve and then sent them out.

Legacy isn't what you build. It's who you equip.

Don't wait until the end of your ministry to start thinking about succession. Start now. Train them. Trust them. And when the time comes, release them with joy.

One thing I often tell young planters is this:

"You may have moved to your town or city—but JESUS died

for your town or city. Follow HIS voice, because He gave His life so that your city can truly live. HE WON'T LET YOU DOWN!"

You absolutely need clear processes and strong structure. You need to build a great team. But above all else, you must focus on health—because healthy bodies grow.

Pastor Anthony Milas Grant United Church

4. Document the Vision

What's in your heart needs to be written down. It's true—there's something powerful about putting your heart on paper. The dreams, the burdens, the lessons God teaches us—they don't belong trapped in our minds where they can be forgotten. They're meant to be shared, passed on, built upon. But if I can be honest, this is one of my weakest areas. Writing things down has never come naturally to me. I tend to carry everything inside—messages, ideas, convictions—but I don't always stop long enough to record them.

It's not because I don't value what's in my heart. I just don't have a great habit of capturing it. Life moves fast. Ministry moves fast. And I tell myself I'll remember, that I'll write it down later, but too often… I don't.

Yet I'm learning that writing is more than documentation—it's discipleship. It's stewardship. If God puts something in my heart, maybe it's not just for me. Maybe it's for the next generation, the people I'm training, or even someone I'll never meet who just needs the encouragement or direction I've already been given.

So I'm learning to pause. To write. Even if it's messy. Even if it's not perfect. Because if I don't write it down, it might be lost. And maybe what feels like my weakest link could become one of the strongest tools God uses—not just in my life, but in the lives of others.

Capture:
- Mission, values, and DNA
- Systems and structures
- Lessons learned
- Practices that protect the vision

This helps future leaders build well.

5. Develop a Leadership Culture

Legacy comes from developing people, not just filling roles.
Legacy comes from developing people, not just filling roles. Anyone can assign a title or a task, but true impact comes when we pour ourselves into others and watch them grow into their God-given calling. As I write this book, I'm not speaking from theory—I'm in the middle of it. I'm actively training and discipling leaders, walking with them, coaching them not just to serve well, but to multiply themselves by creating and coaching their own leaders. It's a beautiful process, but I won't pretend it's easy. In fact, it can be especially daunting when the leaders you're trying to coach aren't quite the right fit—when they're not teachable, not spiritually mature, or simply not ready. That's when discouragement can creep in. But even then, I've learned not to abandon the process. Instead, I keep investing, keep praying, and keep looking for those faithful, available, and teachable hearts—because legacy isn't built overnight, and it's certainly not built by accident. It's built by intentional discipleship and the slow, steady work of reproducing leaders who can carry the mission forward long after I'm gone.

- Identify potential early
- Invite young people into leadership
- Offer internships or residencies
- Teach theology and spiritual leadership often

Leadership development bridges vision to legacy.

6. Empower Others to Dream

Legacy leaders help others fulfill their God-given dreams.

Ask:
- What dreams are in my leaders' hearts?
- How can I bless and release them?

Celebrate when people outgrow your plans for them. That's legacy.

7. Build Beyond Your Name

Make sure:
- Others preach, lead, and make decisions
- The church thrives without your constant presence
- The spotlight is on the team, not just you

Let what you build point to Jesus — not to you.

8. Think in Generations

Don't just plan for the next few years — plan for decades.
- Invest deeply in children and youth
- Equip families for spiritual leadership
- Encourage older generations to mentor younger ones
- Preserve and tell stories of God's faithfulness

Legacy is generational.

9. Stay Rooted in the Gospel

Trends fade. Styles change. But the gospel endures.

Keep legacy anchored in:
- The Word of God
- The lordship of Jesus
- The power of the Spirit
- The Great Commission

10. Finish Well

Legacy isn't just how you build — it's how you finish.

Finish with:
- Integrity
- Gratitude
- Humility
- Generosity

Let people say:
"He made disciples. He raised leaders. He pointed to Jesus."

Summary:
Legacy Is What Outlives You
Your name may fade. Your buildings may one day fall. But if you've made disciples and raised leaders, your impact will echo into eternity.

"I have no greater joy than to hear that my children are walking in the truth."
— 3 John 1:4, ESV

Reflection Questions
- If I stepped away today, what would continue?
- Who am I mentoring for the future?
- What values or systems need to be documented?
- Am I building for success today or significance over time?
- What do I want my spiritual legacy to be?

CHAPTER 15

MAINTAINING UNITY ACROSS CHURCHES

When your church becomes a church-planting movement, unity becomes your lifeline.

One of the clearest biblical examples of unity fueling a church-planting movement is found in the church at Antioch. This was a diverse, Spirit-led, mission-minded church, made up of people from different ethnicities and backgrounds—yet deeply unified. Their unity wasn't surface-level—it was built on prayer, fasting, and shared vision. When the Holy Spirit spoke and said, "Set apart for me Barnabas and Saul for the work to which I have called them," the church didn't argue, divide, or hesitate. They responded in one accord. They laid hands on them, sent them out, and supported the work of planting churches across the known world. That single moment sparked Paul's missionary journeys, which led to dozens of church plants and set a global movement in motion.

What made that possible? Unity. They had one heart, one mind, and one mission. They trusted each other. They trusted the Holy Spirit. And they didn't cling to their best leaders—they released them for the sake of the Kingdom.

Without unity:

Think about the way your body works when you're hungry.

Your eyes see the food. Your hand reaches for it. Your fingers grip the fork or spoon. Your arm lifts it to your mouth. Your mouth receives it, chews, and swallows. Every part plays its role without arguing, without seeking recognition, without hesitation. Why? Because they are all part of one body, working together toward one goal: nourishment and life.

Now imagine if your hand refused to cooperate. Imagine if it said, "Why should I serve the mouth? I want the food for myself." Or if the arm got tired of lifting and decided to rest instead. You'd go hungry. The whole body would suffer—not just the mouth.

That's the kind of unity a church-planting movement needs. Every person, every leader, every church must know their role and be willing to serve the greater mission, not just their individual preferences. When unity is present, the movement grows in health, strength, and multiplication. When it's absent, even the strongest vision can starve. Unity isn't optional—it's vital.

- Vision blurs.
- Trust erodes.
- Churches drift apart.

With unity:
- Churches stay strong, joyful, and mission-focused — even across locations and leaders.

The Underground Church in China

The house church movement in China is one of the most significant examples of unity sustaining a church-planting explosion under intense pressure. For decades, government opposition made traditional church structures impossible. But instead of collapsing, the church went underground—and multiplied. Why? Because of unity.

These churches had no denominational structure, no budgets, no buildings, and often no trained pastors. What they did have was a deep, Spirit-formed unity around the core essentials: the authority of Scripture, the lordship of Jesus, and the mission to make disciples who make disciples. Leaders trusted each other, shared resources, and worked together in secret networks. They didn't compete. They didn't care who got the credit. They cared about seeing people saved and churches planted in every village and city—even if it cost them everything. That unity became their lifeline. Without it, the movement would've fractured under persecution. With it, they became one of the fastest-growing church movements in the world.

> *"Make every effort to maintain the unity of the Spirit in the bond of peace."*
> — Ephesians 4:3, ESV

Unity doesn't mean uniformity. It means shared heart, shared mission, and mutual commitment.

1. Prioritize Relationships Over Structure

Systems matter — but unity is built on relationships.

I once served under a pastor who, rather than celebrating the fruit of ministry, became increasingly jealous of the work God was doing through me. At first, I tried to ignore it, assuming it would pass. But over time, his insecurity began to surface in harmful ways. He would subtly stir up division between me and other leaders, question my motives, and create confusion that damaged relationships. What hurt the most wasn't the personal attacks—it was seeing how that spirit of competition and mistrust disrupted the unity of the church. People were caught in the crossfire. Momentum was lost. The mission suffered. I learned a hard but important truth: leadership that isn't secure in its calling can become a threat to the very thing it's trying to build. And when ego replaces unity, the whole body feels it.

That experience taught me a principle I carry with me to this day: secure leaders empower others; insecure leaders compete with them. If we're going to multiply the Kingdom, we must be leaders who lift others up, not hold them back. We can't afford to let jealousy, pride, or control creep into our leadership—it poisons the culture and stunts the growth of the church. Unity doesn't mean uniformity, and it certainly doesn't mean insecurity. It means celebrating each other's gifts, recognizing that we are on the same team, and remembering that the mission is bigger than any one person. When we choose humility and honor over competition, the church becomes a place where leaders thrive, disciples multiply, and Jesus is glorified.

- Schedule regular check-ins between pastors and leaders.
- Gather for retreats, conferences, or prayer nights.
- Share meals, stories, and struggles.
- Celebrate wins together.
- Pray for and with one another.

Relational glue holds movements together.

Relational glue holds movements together. It's not just structure, strategy, or vision that sustains multiplication—it's trust. Relationships are the invisible thread that keeps leaders aligned, teams unified, and churches working as one body. In any church-planting movement, there will be pressure, misunderstandings, spiritual attacks, and logistical chaos. What keeps everything from falling apart in those moments isn't the brilliance of your systems—it's the strength of your relationships. When leaders genuinely love one another, prefer one another, and communicate with honesty and humility, that bond becomes the glue that holds the whole thing together. But when relationships break down, the movement begins to fracture—no matter how exciting the vision may be. That's why investing in trust, integrity, and open communication isn't optional for movement leaders. It's essential. Relational unity isn't just a nice byproduct of ministry—it's what gives the movement its staying power.

Habits That Strengthen Relational Glue Among Leaders:

1. Pray together regularly. Shared prayer builds spiritual unity like nothing else. When leaders seek God together, hearts align, walls fall down, and the Spirit leads.
2. Talk it out early. Don't let small offenses grow into silent divisions. If something feels off, bring it into the light. Early conversations save relationships.
3. Celebrate one another. Publicly honor others' wins. Jealousy dies when you choose to cheer instead of compare.
4. Pursue authenticity, not performance. Movements thrive

when leaders are real with each other. Share your weaknesses, not just your highlights. Be human.

5. Practice mutual submission. True unity means nobody clings to control. Yield to each other. Trust each other. Be more concerned with the mission than your own position.

6. Break bread often. Eat together. Laugh together. Build friendships outside of meetings and ministry. It's hard to divide from someone you genuinely love.

7. Guard the culture. Protect the tone of the team. Call out gossip. Shut down competition. Keep the atmosphere clean, humble, and honoring.

According to Association of Baptists for World Evangelism (AWBE) Globally, 71% of missionaries who return home each year leave the field for preventable reasons. What might be the biggest factor? We believe it all comes down to team dynamics.

https://abwe.org/blog/team-conflict-number-one-reason-missionaries-go-home/

2. Repeat Vision and Values Often

Vision leaks over time. Keep it fresh by:
- Teaching core values and mission regularly.
- Sharing a common discipleship process.
- Repeating unifying statements like: "One church in many communities, reaching people with the gospel."

"Write the vision; make it plain... so he may run who reads it."
— Habakkuk 2:2, ESV

Repetition brings alignment.

3. Empower Local Expression

Unity doesn't require sameness.

Let each church:
- Shape worship and service styles that fit their context.
- Choose service times that serve their community.
- Develop ministries that meet local needs.

Encourage creativity within shared vision and theology.

4. Stay Theologically Aligned

Doctrinal unity is non-negotiable.
- Share a statement of faith across all churches.
- Offer regular theological training for leaders.
- Address drift with grace and clarity.
- Protect core gospel truths at all costs.

5. Create Rhythms of Connection

Healthy networks stay connected through:
- Monthly leadership calls
- Quarterly network prayer nights
- Annual retreats for renewal and vision
- Shared devotionals or series during key seasons

Connection doesn't happen by accident. Plan for it.

6. Handle Conflict Biblically

Conflict will come. How you handle it defines your unity.
- Address issues directly and lovingly.
- Seek understanding before judgment.
- Bring in mediation when needed.
- Pursue peace over personal victory.

"If possible, so far as it depends on you, live peaceably with all."

— Romans 12:18, ESV

7. Share Resources Generously

Unity grows through shared generosity.
- Contribute to common planting funds.
- Share graphics, sermons, or admin tools.
- Lend support during key seasons or crises.

When one church wins, the whole network wins.

In the kingdom of God, success is not meant to be isolated. The church is not a collection of competitors, but a family of co-laborers. When one church grows, reaches the lost, makes disciples, plants new works, or sees breakthrough after years of faithfulness — that victory doesn't belong to them alone. It belongs to all of us.

We are members of one body. A win for one part strengthens the whole.Every Wednesday at 3 PM, we gather with our pastors for a time of encouragement, vision, and alignment. These meetings are more than just updates and logistics — they're moments to remind each other why we do what we do. I often tell them, "Every time we win — whether it's through a Vacation Bible School, a kids camp, a soccer tournament, or a local outreach — that is a win for the kingdom of heaven."

These aren't small events or side activities. They are seeds of transformation. A child hears the gospel for the first time. A parent shows up to a soccer game and encounters the love of Christ. A whole family is impacted by a single moment of ministry. These aren't just wins for a single church — they are kingdom wins. Eternal wins.

And here's what happens when we keep winning: the church grows. Disciples are made. New leaders are identified. Young people who encounter Jesus in these events find themselves drawn into deeper discipleship, many eventually enrolling in the Bible college. And from that Bible college, we are training up the next wave of pastors, missionaries, and church planters.

It's all connected. Each event matters. Each soul matters.

So I remind our pastors often: don't ever underestimate what God can do through a simple act of faithfulness. That VBS might produce the next church planter. That soccer outreach could spark a movement. These wins build momentum — and that momentum pushes the mission forward.

And through that mission, we will plant more churches.

Because this isn't about building one ministry — it's about multiplying the kingdom.

When a small rural congregation baptizes its first convert in months, heaven rejoices — and so should we. When a new church plant survives the difficult first year, it becomes a beacon of hope for others still struggling. When a church in one part of the world pioneers a new missions strategy, the entire network gains a tool that can be multiplied. When a persecuted house church stands firm under pressure, their faith fuels courage in others.

In a healthy church-planting movement or mission network, we celebrate together, grieve together, and grow together. There is no room for jealousy or competition when we understand the nature of spiritual family. One church's breakthrough is a down payment on another's future. One answered prayer builds faith across borders. One testimony of healing, salvation, or restoration reminds every pastor and planter that God is still working.

We don't win alone. And we don't lose alone either. That's the beauty of the body of Christ.

So let's learn to cheer each other on, share what we've learned, and lift each other up. Because when one church wins, the whole network wins. And when the network wins, the kingdom advances.

8. Tell the Story Again and Again

There is life changing power in the story of Jesus. Trailhead international President Brain Weed if often quoted saying " I believe without a doubt heaven is real, hell is real, and we have to do something about that." What he's referring to is telling the story of Jesus to every tribe and nation and tongue in the world.

Stories unite hearts.
- Share testimonies of salvations, baptisms, and breakthroughs.
- Celebrate new church plants and answered prayers.
- Use newsletters, videos, or pulpit swaps to spread the good news.

What you celebrate becomes part of your culture.

It's important—crucial even—that you learn to genuinely celebrate the wins in the lives of the people you're working with. In a church-planting movement, you're surrounded by leaders running hard after God, making disciples, and sometimes seeing incredible fruit. When those you've discipled begin to rise, when God starts blessing their ministry, giving them influence, favor, or results, you have a choice to make. You can celebrate them—or you can compete with them. That choice will define the health of your heart and the future of your team. Jealousy is a subtle enemy that can creep in when you see others succeed in the very areas you've been working so hard in. But if you're secure in your identity and calling, you'll rejoice instead of resent. You'll see their fruit as part of your fruit. Their victory as a win for the Kingdom. Movements don't multiply through comparison—they multiply through celebration. Be the kind of leader who shouts louder for someone else's breakthrough than your own. That's what keeps your heart clean and your culture healthy.

When I first moved to Africa, one of the most striking things I noticed early on had nothing to do with buildings, language, or even ministry structures—it was the way people celebrated. Whether it was a football match or a local competition, it didn't matter which team lost. When the final whistle blew, everyone would cheer for the winners. Even the losing side joined in, singing, dancing, and celebrating as if they had won themselves. That kind of culture hit me deeply. It revealed a mindset I believe is crucial for Kingdom work: the ability to celebrate others even when the victory isn't yours. In ministry, this attitude is rare but powerful. When we can genuinely rejoice in the success of others—when another church grows, another leader is raised up, or another team sees fruit—that's when we know our hearts are aligned with Heaven. Because in the Kingdom, one person's win is a win for us all.

9. Define What Holds You Together

Be clear on your shared commitments:
- Doctrinal alignment
- Leadership covenants
- Multiplication goals
- Shared financial investment in planting

Put it in writing — for clarity, not control.

10. Keep the Gospel at the Center

Strategies may vary. Styles will differ. But the gospel unites.

Across the world, churches approach ministry in different ways. Some gather in cathedrals, others under trees. Some rely on liturgy and tradition, while others embrace spontaneity and simplicity. One pastor may emphasize teaching, while another focuses on community outreach. Methods evolve. Cultural contexts shape expressions. Personalities bring color to ministry.

But in the midst of all this diversity, there is one unchanging center: the gospel of Jesus Christ.

The gospel is not a style. It is not a method. It is not bound to a denomination, a nation, or a generation. It is the good news that Jesus Christ died for our sins, was buried, and rose again — offering forgiveness, reconciliation, and eternal life to all who believe.

This message has the power to transcend languages, traditions, and preferences. It unites believers from every tribe and tongue into one body. It compels missionaries to go, churches to send, and disciples to multiply. No matter how different our methods or ministry models may be, if the gospel is at the center, we are working together toward the same goal.

So let us celebrate our diversity without losing our unity. Let us be creative without compromising truth. Let us adapt our strategies while holding fast to the message.

Because in the end, it's not about how we go — it's about who we go for.

"Is Christ divided?"

— 1 Corinthians 1:13, ESV

Keep Jesus at the center — and unity will follow.

When my family and I were serving in the Philippines, I had the opportunity to observe two very different types of missionaries working in the same region. One missionary stood out because of his generosity of spirit. He was the kind of leader who celebrated your wins as if they were his own. Whether you were just getting started or had been in the field for years, he would take time to mentor you, encourage you, and speak life into your calling. Even on the days when things didn't go well, he was there—not with criticism, but with grace and wisdom. His ministry was thriving—not because he was flashy or controlling, but because he was kingdom-minded. In fact, it grew to become the largest and most fruitful mission ministry I had ever seen. On the other hand, there was another missionary who operated in a completely different spirit. He was always anxious about someone else doing better than him, constantly guarding his ideas, suspicious of anyone who might "steal" his influence. His ministry, though inherited from someone else, remained small, stagnant, and structurally weak. There was no vision, no real unity, and no culture of collaboration. What I learned from that contrast is this: insecurity kills momentum, but a spirit of celebration and mentorship multiplies it. The most fruitful leaders are those who don't compete, but invest in others and open doors for them to thrive.

Summary:

One Body, Many Locations

A church-planting movement isn't measured by the number of churches — but by the strength of their connection in love and mission.

Keep relationships strong. Keep theology sound. Keep hearts humble. And your movement will not just grow — it will endure.

"How good and pleasant it is when brothers dwell in unity!"
— Psalm 133:1, ESV

Reflection Questions
- Are our churches relationally connected — or drifting apart?
- What rhythms can we build to strengthen unity?
- How do we maintain theological alignment as we grow?
- Are we telling the story and celebrating together?

CONCLUSION:

THE CALL TO MULTIPLY

Church planting is not just a strategy — it's a response to the Great Commission.

From the first chapter to this final word, we've walked through the foundations, struggles, and systems needed to start not just one church, but many. In the end, it's not about numbers. It's about obedience. It's about hearing God's voice and saying, 'Yes.'

Living in God's supernatural plan is both terrifying and rewarding. It stretches you, tests you, and teaches you dependence on Him. Yes — you'll face doubt. Yes — you'll wonder at times why you started. But when you see God's hand in every detail, you'll know: this work will impact generations yet unborn.

At the heart of it all, it comes down to this: hearing the voice of God—and saying yes.

There's nothing like living in the supernatural flow of God's plan. It's not easy. It's often scary. It demands sacrifice, hard work, and a willingness to walk into the unknown. But it's also where the impossible becomes possible—where you witness God do what only He can do.

There will be moments of doubt. You'll question your decision. You'll wonder why you started down this path in the first place. But stay the course. Keep saying yes. Because when the dust settles and the work is done, you'll look back and see God in every detail—every provision, every open door, every miracle.

And in that moment, you'll realize something greater: your obedience wasn't just about today. It was about generations to come. Your yes will echo beyond your lifetime, impacting lives and shaping destinies that haven't even begun yet.

"And your ears shall hear a word behind you, saying, 'This is the way, walk in it,' when you turn to the right or when you turn to the left" (Isaiah 30:21, ESV).

When you follow God's voice, you're not just building something temporary. You're stepping into a legacy that will outlive you.

"The harvest is plentiful, but the laborers are few; therefore, pray earnestly to the Lord of the harvest to send out laborers into his harvest." — Luke 10:2, ESV

You are that laborer. Your team is that answer. Your church is that miracle in motion.

This Is a Kingdom Movement

You're not building an empire. You're building God's Kingdom.

Every soul saved.
Every leader equipped.
Every disciple made.
Every neighborhood reached.
Every church planted.

It all matters. And it all begins again — with your next yes.

You Were Made for This

You may not feel qualified. You may wonder if you have enough people, resources, or support. But remember: God doesn't call the equipped. He equips the called.

You were made to multiply.

You were made to send.
You were made to lead with faith, prayer, and love.

This journey will stretch you — and it will shape you. The Kingdom will expand because of it.

Keep Going

There will be days you want to quit.
Keep going.

There will be seasons of uncertainty and pain.
Keep going.

There will be victories worth celebrating — and trials worth enduring.
Keep going.

One day, you'll look back and realize: God used you to change lives, plant churches, and multiply His Kingdom. And it was all worth it.

Final Prayer

Father, thank You for calling us into Your harvest. Thank You for entrusting us with Your Church. Strengthen every leader reading this. Fill them with courage, wisdom, and bold obedience.

May their lives and ministries bring You glory. May their churches multiply disciples, leaders, and love. And may the name of Jesus be lifted high in every city, every community, and every nation.

In Jesus' name, Amen.

ENDNOTES

1. Roland Allen, The Spontaneous Expansion of the Church (Grand Rapids: Eerdmans, 1962), 7.
Allen describes how the Spirit empowers believers for natural church multiplication without elaborate structures.

2. David Garrison, Church Planting Movements (Midlothian, VA: WIGTake Resources, 2004), 21.
Garrison defines a church planting movement as a rapid and multiplicative increase of indigenous churches planting churches.

3. George Patterson, Church Multiplication Guide (Pasadena: William Carey Library, 1993), 45.
Patterson emphasizes obedience-based discipleship as essential for true multiplication, not mere accumulation of knowledge.

4. J.D. Payne, Apostolic Church Planting (Downers Grove: IVP, 2015), 16.
Payne calls church planters to focus on starting multiplying movements, not isolated churches.

5. Steve Addison, Movements That Change the World (Downers Grove: IVP, 2011), 43.
Addison highlights characteristics of movements: white-hot faith, commitment to a cause, contagious relationships, rapid mobilization, and adaptive methods.

6. Neil Cole, Organic Church (San Francisco: Jossey-Bass, 2005), 53.
Cole reminds us that the church is people living on mission, not buildings or events.

7. Alan Hirsch, The Forgotten Ways (Grand Rapids: Brazos Press, 2006), 34.
Hirsch urges recovering the early church's apostolic DNA for rapid multiplication.

8.   David Watson and Paul Watson, Contagious Disciple Making (Nashville: Thomas Nelson, 2014), 59.
The Watsons advocate for simple, obedience-based disciple-making that fuels movements of church planting.

The quote from E.M. Bounds—"Our praying needs to be pressed and pursued with an energy that never tires, a persistency which will not be denied, and a courage that never fails"—is taken from his influential book Power Through Prayer (first published in 1910).

Christian author Randy Alcorn once said, *"Our eternal investment portfolio should be full of the most strategic kingdom-building projects to which we can disburse God's funds."*[1] [1] Randy Alcorn, Money, Possessions, and Eternity (Tyndale House Publishers), quoted via AZQuotes.

ACKNOWLEDGMENTS

No one plants a church — let alone six in twelve months — alone.

This journey has been marked by partnership, prayer, sacrifice, and love. I'm deeply grateful for everyone who has stood with me in the call to multiply the Kingdom.

To my family — thank you for believing in the mission and walking with me through every high and low. Your support has been my foundation.

To my wife — your patience, wisdom, and prayers have sustained me more than words can say.

To my mentors and spiritual parents — thank you for sowing into me, speaking truth, and modeling faithful leadership.

To our core teams and every church member who said "yes" — you are the true heroes of this Kingdom story.

To our church planters, staff, and volunteers — thank you for sacrificing for the gospel and building something that will outlast us all.

To partnering churches, networks, and donors — your investment is bearing fruit far beyond what you can see.

And to Jesus Christ — our Shepherd, Cornerstone, and Head. All we've done is because of You, and for You.

To God be all the glory.

www.ingramcontent.com/pod-product-compliance
Lightning Source LLC
Chambersburg PA
CBHW072003040426
42447CB00009B/1458